CITY TO THE
BLACK
COUNTRY

CITY TO THE BLACK COUNTRY

A NOSTALGIC JOURNEY BY BUS & TRAM

DAVID HARVEY

First published 2009

The History Press
The Mill, Brimscombe Port
Stroud, Gloucestershire, GL5 2QG
www.thehistorypress.co.uk

ISBN 978 0 7524 5297 5

Typesetting and origination by The History Press
Printed in Great Britain

CONTENTS

	Acknowledgements	6
	Introduction	7
	THE HOCKLEY, HANDSWORTH, THE HAWTHORNS, WEST BROMWICH, CARTER'S GREEN, WEDNESBURY, GREAT BRIDGE AND DUDLEY ROUTE	9
1	Birmingham City Centre	13
2	Constitution Hill to Hockley	27
3	Handsworth to the Boundary	41
4	Football Specials to West Bromwich and Carter's Green	55
5	On to Wednesbury	75
6	What Might Have Been the Route to Wolverhampton	81
7	Carter's Green to Dudley	87
	THE CAPE HILL, SMETHWICK, OLDBURY AND DUDLEY ROUTE	93
8	Birmingham City Centre	97
9	Summer Hill to the Cape of Good Hope	107
10	Cape Hill to Smethwick	117
11	St Paul's Road to Oldbury	125
12	Brades Village to Dudley	139
13	Dudley	145

ACKNOWLEDGEMENTS

The author is grateful to the many photographers acknowledged in the text who have contributed to this volume. Special thanks are due to to my wife Diana for her splendid proofreading. Thanks also to Steve Calder for his invaluable assistance, to Richard Weaver for his advice on the Smethwick section of the book, and to Barry Ware for his informative comments. Roger Smith's excellent maps are wonderfully informative and help the reader to place the photographs in their correct location. The book would not have been possible without the continued encouragement given by Amy Rigg and Emily Locke of the History Press.

INTRODUCTION

Take a journey by public transport along two of the main roads out of Birmingham which lead to Dudley. Today the road by way of West Bromwich is the A41 while the road through Smethwick is the A457, but the first is better known as the Soho and Holyhead Roads while the latter comprises a number of different names but in tram days was always known as 'The Track'. Both routes started in the centre of Birmingham and cross into the Black Country. This cradle of the eighteenth-century Industrial Revolution encompasses an amorphous area which in August 2009 the Ordnance Survey decided to mark on their 1:50,000 scale map, only to find that its boundaries were almost impossible to define!

The first route, on leaving Birmingham City Centre by way of Snow Hill and Constitution Hill, skirted the famous 'Jewellery Quarter' and descended into the industrial area of Hockley centred on the steeply-sided valley of Hockley Brook. This was, at the time of the introduction of public transport, the northern-most part of Birmingham. Although hardly a suburb, it was developed throughout the nineteenth century as an area of heavy industry, and tightly packed back-to-back houses and terraces were served by their own shopping centre. It was at Hockley Brook that the CBT inner cable met the outer second cable, and the cable trams had to coast the few yards from one cable to the other in order to pick up the tow for the second part of their journey. Hockley Depot was located here in Whitmore Street.

Across the boundary, on top of the plateau beyond Soho Hill, is Handsworth. This one-time prosperous area with suburban tree-lined roads and large Victorian villas was a large UDC with its own impressive Town Hall until it was absorbed, under protest, into Birmingham on 9 November 1911. Continuing the climb up the hill through Handsworth, the important Crocketts Lane crossroads dominated by the New Inns at the start of Holyhead Road was reached. Beyond this was the bleak heathland plateau which marked the boundary at West Bromwich, which is straddled by the Hawthorns football ground of West Bromwich Albion, which was first inhabited by the 'Baggies' in 1900.

Into the Black Country, the town of West Bromwich stood at the far end of Sandwell Valley. The town had a population of 137,000 at the 2001 census. The town's main high street is today largely pedestrianised from Dartmouth Square almost to the late Victorian Town Hall, but in the days when traffic drove through the centre of town, this was known as the Golden Mile because of the quality of its excellent shopping centre. At the northern end of West Bromwich is Carter's Green, dominated by the Farley Clock Tower.

It was at Carter's Green that the two routes split, with the fork to the right leading into the heart of the Black Country's heavy industry area by way of Hill Top. Wednesbury, lying near to the Tame Valley, was one of the world's largest producers of iron and steel tubes, but had suffered severely from the decline in heavy industry after the First World War. The route continued to Darlaston which had a thriving gun, lock, nuts and bolts industry as well as having the South Staffordshire Tram Depot and, of course, a busy Victorian shopping centre. Beyond this the route proceeded to Wolverhampton. In 1971 the through bus service from Birmingham was at last opened, completing the tramway link which from 1912 to 1924 actually got as far as Bilston from Birmingham, but which never reached Wolverhampton.

The left fork from Carter's Green went to the market town of Great Bridge and then underneath the Ryland Canal aqueduct and mainline railway line at Dudley Port before climbing to Burnt Tree where the other tramline from Oldbury was met.

The second route left Birmingham from behind the splendour of the Council House, but it too, once leaving the central area, entered an area of brass foundries, the southern edge of the 'Jewellery Quarter' and some of the most tightly packed back-to-back houses in Birmingham. Having climbed Spring Hill, with the entrance to Rosebery Street Tram Depot/Bus Garage on the right, the route crossed the Birmingham Canal and passed into Dudley Road where the hospital, now called City Hospital, is located. Crossing the long Lee Bridge above the deep cutting over both the Birmingham Canal and the mainline railway line between Birmingham and Wolverhampton, the route went past the only lung of greenery on Dudley Road within the Birmingham boundary. This was Summerfield Park, originally opened in 1876, which was opposite Winson Green Road, a road leading directly to Winson Green Prison. From the park it was just over 1 mile along Dudley Road to the Birmingham-Smethwick boundary at Grove Lane. Just over the Smethwick border was the massive Mitchells & Butlers Brewery, opened on Cape Hill in July 1879 and surviving until December 2002.

The long, steep climb up Cape Hill continued until the junction with Windmill Lane was reached, where a five-way crossroad was the focus of a very large, prosperous Victorian-built shopping centre. Here the tram and later bus services turned off into Waterloo Road towards Bearwood. The main road through Smethwick became High Street at the top of 'The Cape', and proceeded down Bearwood Hill, passing Victoria Park and the Council House, before arriving at the junction of Rolfe Street where there is another important railway station on the former LNWR Stour Valley line to Wolverhampton.

The route continued through another late nineteenth-century shopping area until the end of High Street was reached at St Paul's Road. From here the road passed by Telford's magnificent Galton Bridge and the world famous Chance's huge glassworks before reaching the former Birmingham & Midland Tramways Depot at West Smethwick. This was on the boundary with Oldbury, and today, between the old depot site and Oldbury town centre, the A457 is dwarfed by the concrete pillars and decking of the M5 motorway which strides across this part of the Black Country.

Oldbury's narrow Birmingham Street was negotiated with difficulty before the Market Place and the Council House in Freeth Street were reached. Today the area is dominated by the huge Sava Shopping Centre which opened in the 1980s. Once out of Oldbury on the A457, the road passes through Brades Village which, until recently, was dominated by tracts of derelict industrial land, but has been regenerated with town houses since the late 1990s. Finally the road forked left opposite the site of the long-demolished Boat Inn and climbed over the Birmingham Canal Bridge, into Dudley Road West and through Tividale where the long-forgotten tram works of the Birmingham & Midland Tramways was located. From here it was but a short distance before the aforementioned Burn Tree Junction was met, where the Birmingham New Road, (A4123), built in the mid-1920s to provide employment for the many men laid off from the declining heavy and primary Black Country industries, cut a swathe between Hagley Road West in Birmingham and Wolverhampton. Beyond Burnt Tree Junction the two routes terminated in Dudley (population 195,000), with its historic Market Place, world famous zoo, the Black Country Living Museum and on top of Castle Hill, overlooking the town, the partially ruined Norman castle which had been home to the Earls of Dudley until they moved out of the town to the eighteenth-century Palladian-style Himley Hall near Wombourne.

This book takes both of these two routes between Birmingham and Dudley and examines both historic and modern street scenes, their geographic location and their social history.

David Harvey
Dudley, April 2009

THE HOCKLEY, HANDSWORTH, THE HAWTHORNS, WEST BROMWICH, CARTER'S GREEN, WEDNESBURY, GREAT BRIDGE AND DUDLEY ROUTE

The first tram route to run within Birmingham was that operated by the Birmingham & District Co. when, on 11 September 1873, they opened a standard-gauge horse tramline from Monmouth Street (Colmore Row) to Hockley Brook. This met the same company's 4ft 8½in lines from outside the Birmingham City boundary coming from Dudley Port and Hill Top as far as Hockley Brook, which had opened even earlier on Whit Monday 20 May 1872. The Handsworth section as far as the New Inns continued to be used for the next decade, but the West Bromwich sections were gradually abandoned by about 1874.

The South Staffordshire & Birmingham District Steam Tramway Co. opened a 3ft 6in gauge steam tramway from the New Inns, Handsworth through West Bromwich, Wednesbury to Darlaston on 16 July 1883. Meanwhile, the Birmingham Central Tramways (BCT), through their parent company, had entered into an agreement with the Patent Cable Tramways Corporation to construct a 3ft 6in cable route. BCT were by this time operating steam trams on seven routes within the town, and one of these, to Great Hampton Row and Wheeler Street, opened on 25 October 1886, would partly overrun the intended cable route as far as the Great Hampton Street and Great Hampton Row junction. This CBT steam tram route was closed on 31 December 1906, leaving the Great Hampton Row tracks unused.

CBT's cable route, given a twenty-one-year operating lease, was opened from Colmore Row to Hockley Brook on 24 March 1888, and was operated from a new depot in Hockley. This route was extended on a second cable to the New Inns on 20 April 1889. The Central Co. was taken over by the City of Birmingham Tramways (CBT) on 29 September 1896, and had presumed that they would replace all of their steam, cable and battery trams with overhead electric operation. Local power politics now took over as Birmingham Corporation applied for parliamentary powers to operate its own municipal system, thus empowering them to take over the leases in the city when they expired. Meanwhile, Handsworth UDC purchased the cable car tracks from Hockley Brook to the New Inns boundary.

The South Staffordshire (Lessee) Co. (SS) opened its electric tram route from the Woodman Inn, adjacent to the Hawthorns football ground of West Bromwich Albion on Holyhead Road, to Carter's Green on 19 December 1902, using large open-top Brush-bodied bogie cars. An extension to Great Bridge was opened on 24 January 1903 while the route to Wednesbury was opened on 10 April 1903, replacing the steam tram service except for the short section between the New Inns and Woodman, which linked the ¾-mile gap between the CBT cable tram terminus and the new SS electric terminus. This strange anomaly was finally abandoned on 15 June 1904. After reaching an agreement with Handsworth UDC, the SS Co. extended its service from Woodman to the New Inns on 1 October 1904. On 30 May 1903 the Great Bridge route was extended to Dudley Railway Station, running over the B&M tracks from the Burnt Tree Junction to the terminus.

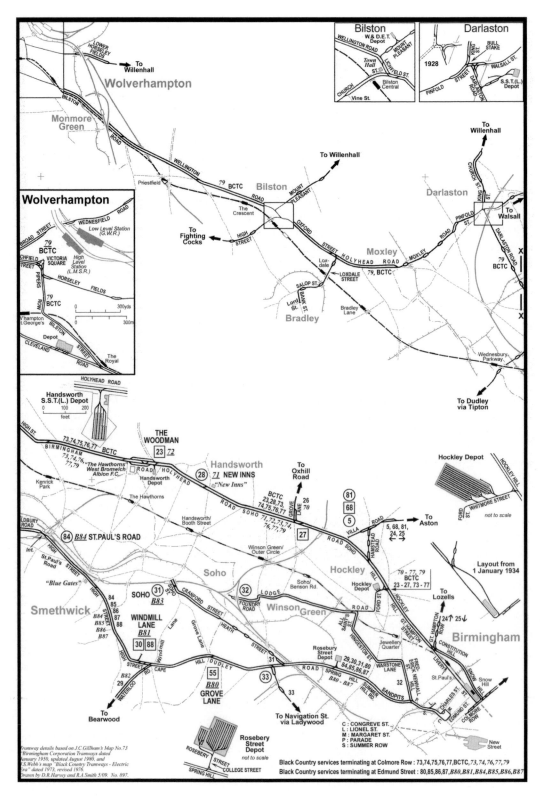

Bilston
W.& D.E.T. Depot
1928

Darlaston

Wolverhampton

To Willenhall

Monmore Green

79 BCTC

Bilston

To Willenhall

Darlaston

To Willenhall

To Walsall

To Fighting Cocks

Moxley

79, BCTC

79 BCTC

Bradley

To Dudley via Tipton

Wolverhampton

Handsworth S.S.T.(L.) Depot

73,74,75,76,77 BCTC
BIRMINGHAM
73,74,76, 77,79

THE WOODMAN
23 72

Handsworth

28 71 NEW INNS

To Oxhill Road

Hockley Depot

BCTC
23,28,73, 74,75,76,77
71,72,73,74, 76,77,79

26 70

81

68

5

27

To Aston

5, 68, 81, 24, 25

84 B84 ST.PAUL'S ROAD

Soho

Hockley

Layout from 1 January 1934

SOHO 31 B83

32

Hockley Depot

70 - 77, 79 BCTC 23 - 27, 73 - 77

To Lozells

24 ↑ 25 ↓

Smethwick

84 85 86 87 88

WINDMILL LANE B81

30 88

Winson Green

Birmingham

55 B80 GROVE LANE

33

B82

To Bearwood

To Navigation St. via Ladywood

Rosebery Street Depot

C : CONGREVE ST.
L : LIONEL ST.
M : MARGARET ST.
P : PARADE
S : SUMMER ROW

Tramway details based on J.C.Gillham's Map No.73
"Birmingham Corporation Tramways dated
January 1950, updated August 1980, and
J.S.Webb's map "Black Country Tramways - Electric
Era" dated 1973, revised 1976.
Drawn by D.R.Harvey and R.A.Smith 5/09. No. 897.

Black Country services terminating at Colmore Row : 73,74,75,76,77,BCTC,73,74,76,77,79
Black Country services terminating at Edmund Street : 80,85,86,87,B80,B81,B84,B85,B86,B87

10

On Friday 30 June 1911 the CBT cable tram route was closed when the leases in Birmingham expired. On the following day BCT began operations over the route and to the Handsworth boundary at the Hawthorns, and the SS trams were once again cut back to the Woodman Inn. Initially BCT began operations using the small Brill open-top cars from the 221 series along with almost brand new 301-class UEC vestibule four-wheelers. These were initially operated by the Miller Street Depot until 12 June 1912 when Hockley re-opened after its conversion from cable to overhead electric operation.

On 9 November 1911 the city was enlarged by the incorporation of Handsworth into Greater Birmingham. One of the first major alterations to the tram services was the introduction of the 'South Staffs Through Cars' on 9 October 1912 from Darlaston using route-branded top-covered 'Aston'-type four-wheelers. Further BCT branches within the city were opened, with the former steam tram route to Lozells reopening on 12 November 1912, Oxhill Road on 20 December 1912 and Hamstead Road on 6 January 1913. In addition a single loop around Snow Hill Station using Livery Street was opened on 11 June 1913, which all but removed tramcars terminating at Colmore Row.

At the end of 1913 Hockley Depot received thirty of the new UEC-built open-balconied bogie cars from the 512–586-class to operate on the Soho Road routes. The delivery in 1920 of similar-looking Brush-built trams, numbered 612–636, released older tramcars, but the acquisition on 1 April 1924 of the routes to West Bromwich, Carter's Green, Wednesbury and Dudley left Hockley very short of bogie cars. As a result, in the following year the rest of the 1920 Brush-built trams, 587–611, went to Hockley. In 1926 new air-brake bogie cars were sent to Rosebery Street to operate the Ladywood 33 service along Icknield Port Road, allowing cars 512–535 to join the other members of their class already at Hockley. From 1926 until 1931 the large bogie cars were all modernised by having their balconies enclosed, receiving upholstered seating and being re-motored with either 63 or 70hp engines.

The West Bromwich Lease was due to expire on 31 March 1924 and an agreement was made to operate Birmingham Corporation trams over the boundary through West Bromwich and on to Wednesbury and Dudley. There was a suggestion that BCT could run over SS tracks to Darlaston and Bilston, and a Hockley bogie car actually reached Bilston. Unfortunately the projected BCT-operated 'Black Country Through Cars' never happened because BCT considered the state of the tram tracks to be poor and would not countenance running their trams using side-mounted overheads. The Black Country Through Service was closed at this time as well. As a result, for a few years, at The White Horse terminus, Birmingham and Walsall Corporation trams and South Staffordshire trams all terminated within yards of each other, with sections of unconnected track remaining in the gap between the three lines.

In May 1937, with the West Bromwich Lease about to come to an end, the latter Corporation proposed a take over of the running of the services with jointly operated trolleybuses. Birmingham, although a trolleybus operator, insisted on joint motorbus operation despite West Bromwich rebuilding Oak Lane Garage's entrance to a greater height in order to accommodate trolleybus overheads. BCT wanted to keep open all the Soho Road routes within the city boundary, including the recently relayed Oxhill Road branch, but reluctantly decided on complete closure on 2 April 1939.

The replacement BCT buses were the complete batch of 211–295 EOG-registered Leyland 'Titan' TD6cs, while West Bromwich's share of the joint services were thirty-one Daimler COG6s numbered 71-101. The Birmingham fleet was badly damaged on the night of 19 November 1940 when Hockley Garage was bombed, though within two days services were running almost normally again. The joint operation continued throughout the following thirty years with Hockley gaining the whole of the batch of fifty Leyland-bodied 'Titan' PD2/1s (2131–2180) as well as the first fifteen of the next batch of Park Royal-bodied PD2/1s. West Bromwich Corporation continued to employ a variety of Daimler CVG6s, including the last exposed radiator examples fitted with attractive Weymann bodies delivered in 1952. Hockley eventually received all of the 1962 DOC-registered Leyland 'Atlantean' PDR1/1s, which were mainly for use on the Lodge Road service but were occasionally allowed out on the 72 route to the city boundary at the Hawthorns. In 1965 some Metro Cammell Weyman (MCW)-bodied Daimler 'Fleetlines' were allocated to Hockley, and, just before the takeover by West Midland PTE on 1 October 1969, Hockley Garage received two-door Daimler 'Fleetline' CRG6LXs with Park Royal bodies.

After the PTE takeover, the Dudley and Wednesbury services were jointly operated with Hockley, though more and more the West Bromwich share gradually increased, eventually taking over completely on the closure of Hockley Garage in May 2005. Since the closure of Hockley Garage, whose original 1888 buildings are Grade II listed and saved for posterity, the 74 route is usually operated by West Bromwich Garage and the 79 by Park Lane, Wolverhampton. The 79 service between Birmingham, West Bromwich, Wednesbury, Darlaston and Wolverhampton began operating on 28 February 1971, completing a route whose antecedent was the Black Country Through Service operated by South Staffordshire Tramways. The 75 route to Wednesbury was replaced at this time as it was integrated into the 79 route to Wolverhampton. Many Daimler and Leyland 'Fleetlines', especially those of the YOX –K, NOC-R and SDA-S registered batches, were operated on the route, although during a period of about six years after the takeover there was a delightful mixture of former municipal buses from Birmingham, West Bromwich and Walsall.

Since de-regulation in October 1986 a number of smaller bus companies have operated bus services on the Birmingham to Dudley corridor. These include Birmingham Coach Co., recently reformed again in 2008 as Black Diamond Bus, and before this Pete's Travel, aka Probus, as well as a variety of operators with elderly Leyland Nationals and tiny Dennis Darts being used by their fifth or sixth owners.

The MCW 'Metrobus', especially in its Mk II form, was allocated to both Hockley and West Bromwich garages from the mid-1980s, and were the backbone of the 74 and 79 services until about 2002. The first major change made to the routes through West Bromwich from Birmingham by Travel West Midlands was to replace the 'Metrobuses'. Their long tenure gradually came to a close as new Alexander-bodied Dennis 'Tridents' and Volvo B7TLs were introduced from 2002, and at the time of writing (2009) these buses still provide a good reliable service.

1

BIRMINGHAM
CITY CENTRE

On a miserable afternoon on 22 November 2003, a Travel West Midlands double-decker travels along Corporation Street, working on the 79 route. 4316 (BX 02 ARF), an Alexander-bodied Dennis 'Trident' SFD334, is still showing the Birmingham destination which would shortly be changed to show Wolverhampton. The 79 service was introduced on 28 February 1971 after WMPTE took over bus operations in the West Midlands, replacing the old 75 service to Wednesbury and extending it via Bilston to Wolverhampton. (D.R. Harvey)

Travelling around the newly refurbished Old Square on 8 October 2008 is 4298 (BU 51 RYF). This Volvo B7TL with an Alexander H47/27F body entered service in February 2002. This bus had been allocated to Hockley Garage when new, but after that garage closed on 26 May 2005 it was moved to Perry Barr Garage. The bus was then working on the 74 service from Dudley via West Bromwich which had been extended around the city centre from its original terminus outside Snow Hill Station. Old Square had been rebuilt in the 1960s with a central pedestrian subway, but in 1997 this was filled in and the former Bell, Nicolson & Lunt building on the right was refurbished as Cannon House in 2007. (D.R. Harvey)

196 (MDA 196E) waits at Stephenson Street terminus on the 79 route, still in its original green and yellow Wolverhampton Corporation livery. It stands in the shadow of the ninety-four-unit Birmingham Shopping Centre which was built in February 1972 on a raft of concrete over New Street Station. It was a miserable and much criticised development, being too big, too inaccessible and, worse, reducing the transport hub into a labyrinthine underground railway station. All post-war Guys purchased by Wolverhampton Corporation were fitted with either Wilson pre-selector or semi-automatic gearboxes. Some of the last Guy 'Arab'Vs bought by Wolverhampton had Strachan H41/31F bodies, looking at first sight like products produced by MCW. Unfortunately the Strachan product was very poor, and this particular bus was no exception as it was withdrawn in 1973 after just six years in service. (L. Mason)

After West Midland, PTE took over bus operations in 1969. Some of the bus services using Soho Road were re-routed by way of Colmore Row, New Street, including the 74 route. Passing through Victoria Square in 1987 is MCW 'Metrobus' Mk II 2860 (B860 AOP). With the impressive Council House designed by Yeoville Thomason in 1874 in a Neo-Classical style, this West Bromwich Garage allocated bus is roughly where, since the start of the twenty-first century, the Christmas German Market is located. Victoria Square was completely redesigned in 1995, and included the famous River Goddess statue and fountain, locally known as 'the Floosie in the Jacuzzi', which was opened by the late Diana, Princess of Wales. (R. Buckley)

St Philip's Church was designed by Thomas Archer in 1709. Archer, who had been a pupil of Sir Christopher Wren, was commissioned by the Colmore family to design a church for the wealthier inhabitants of Birmingham. Named St Philip's after one of the Colmore family, the church was completed by 1715, although the Baroque-style tower was not completed for another ten years. The church became the Birmingham Diocese Cathedral Church in 1905 and stands in its own quiet oasis known locally as 'The Churchyard'. Waiting in Colmore Row is a Birmingham Corporation 512-class open-balconied bogie car. The Soho Road tram services had kerbside loading in Colmore Row for just over twenty years. On 4 June 1933 these routes were moved to a new terminus outside the front of Snow Hill Station. (Commercial Postcard)

The impressive frontage of Snow Hill Station was completed as the 120-room Great Western Hotel in 1868. Unfortunately the railway station behind it was a somewhat shabby place until it was rebuilt by the Great Western Railway, opening during January 1912 with a staggeringly huge roof of 12,000 square yards. The old station buildings on the platforms located alongside Livery Street are still visible on the left. In about 1899 a CBT cable tram, car 84, moves along Colmore Row and is about to make the left-hand turn into Snow Hill. This open-top bogie car was built by Falcon in 1888 as part of the original cable car fleet. On the right travelling along Colmore Row towards the cathedral is a horse bus. There are three horses pulling the bus rather than the usual two because of the steepness of Snow Hill. This third horse was known as a trace horse. (Birmingham Central Reference Library)

Working on the 24 route to Lozells via Constitution Hill and Wheeler Street is one of the open-balcony 512-class of bogie cars of which over fifty were allocated to Hockley Depot by the mid-1920s. The tram is loading up at the impressive shelters in Colmore Row alongside St Philip's churchyard. Travelling towards Snow Hill is a Short-bodied AEC 504 working on the 4 route from Queen's Park, Harborne. Behind the tram is the Blue Coat School building which was founded in 1722 by the first rector of St Philip's, William Higgs, to educate children from poor families aged nine to fourteen. The building behind the tram dates from the rebuilding in a four-storey Neo-Classical style in 1794. From 1817 the

school was administered by the Church of England, and, after a series of enlargements, by 1920 the school was recognised as a public elementary school accommodating 250 pupils. A new school was built in Somerset Road, Harborne, in 1930, after which the original building was sold and demolished in 1935. (R.T. Wilson)

A South Staffordshire tramcar stands in Livery Street alongside the refreshment and dining rooms of the Great Western Hotel in about 1920. Open balcony Car 6 was built during the First World War by Birmingham & Midland at their Tividale Works and had a Brush flexible truck and a seating capacity of forty-eight. The tram is working on the Black Country Through Service, and between the decks the tram is carrying the legend 'West Bromwich Wednesbury and Darlaston'. The tram route was opened on 9 October 1912, but this photograph was taken before 26 May 1923 as after this date the route was extended with every other tram going to Bilston. This useful tram service was in many ways the predecessor of West Midlands PTE's 79 bus route between Birmingham and Wolverhampton. (D.R. Harvey Collection)

Some fifteen years later, early in 1914, Birmingham Corporation UEC-bodied sixty-two-seat Car 534, fitted with a Mountain & Gibson Burnley-type maximum traction bogie, entered service as an open balcony tram. In 1927 the car was fitted with a 70hp motor, almost doubling its power making it ideal for the fast running beyond the city boundary as well as having its balconies totally enclosed. The immaculate-looking tram will shortly pull out of Livery Street and turn left to pick up passengers at the shelters in Colmore Row before working on the 28 route to the New Inns public house. (R.T. Wilson)

After the bus conversion of the Handsworth tram routes on 2 April 1939, West Bromwich Corporation, having introduced thirty-one Metro Cammell-bodied Daimler COG5s to the jointly operated services, ordered another four identical buses in May 1939, although they did not enter service until March 1940. These well-constructed vehicles gave the Corporation excellent service, and this bus, 102 (BEA 32), although looking distinctly in need of a repaint, would remain in service until 1957. The bus is standing in front of BCT's 2194 (JOJ 194), an almost new Park Royal-bodied Leyland 'Titan' PD2/1, at the top of Livery Street in about 1951, when working on the 74 route to Dudley. (Travel Lens)

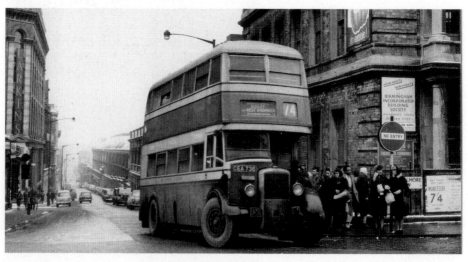

On a miserable day when the snow had all but melted, West Bromwich Corporation 136 (CEA 736), turns out of Livery Street into Colmore Row when working on the 74 service. This bus was one of six Daimler CVD6s which had a rather unusual body design by Metro-Cammell as it was only supplied elsewhere to Chester and Salford Corporations. The registration for this bus had been reserved in late 1946, but it was nearly two years before these vehicles were delivered. Having Daimler CD6 8.6-litre engines, they were not long-lived due to their poor oil consumption and 136 was withdrawn in 1964. (Unknown)

UEC-bodied Car 524, dating from 1914, loads up at the impressive 1930s loading shelters in front of Snow Hill Station in 1939. The tram, dwarfed by both the frontage of Snow Hill Station and the distant General Life building on the corner of Snow Hill and Steelhouse Lane, is working on the 26 route to Oxhill Road. The tram will turn left into Snow Hill as it heads off towards Handsworth. (*Birmingham Post & Mail*)

The roadway in front of the Great Western Railway's Snow Hill Station in Colmore Row was used as part of the anti-clockwise loop via Livery Street, Colmore Row and Snow Hill from 13 June 1913. When the one-way system in the city centre was instigated on 4 June 1933 the termini outside St Philip's Cathedral were abandoned. Brush-bodied 63hp bogie Car 600, built in 1920, is just turning out of the Colmore Row refuge and into Snow Hill as it leaves on the 24 route to Lozells on 31 March 1939. This was the final day of tramway operation on the Handsworth group of tram routes, hence the abandonment notices in the balcony windows. Car 600 was one of only three trams of the 587–636 class to be fitted with an eight-windowed top-deck in 1930. (L.W. Perkins)

Between 5 and 11 May 1926, Birmingham Corporation's tram crews supported the General Strike resulting in very little official public transport operating in Birmingham. During this week, West Bromwich Corporation ran an emergency bus service to Birmingham using volunteer crews. Tilling-Stevens TS3, 5 (EA 999), built in 1920 and fitted with a curiously roofed Roberts B29F body, loads up outside the main entrance to Snow Hill Station in Colmore Row. This bus was the first vehicle in the WBCT fleet to be painted in the blue and deep cream livery. Behind the Tilling-Stevens is the one-year-old fourteen-seat Morris-Commercial, 6 (EA 2370), fitted with a Dixon B14F body. On the right a solitary policeman casts his supervisory role over the proceedings. (WBCT, courtesy of D.F. Potter)

A Ford Eight 7Y, registered in late 1939 in Kingston-upon-Hull, turns into Colmore Row from Bull Street in about 1946 as its driver takes advantage of the policeman's point duty directions. A somewhat battered-looking Snow Hill Station, awaiting a new roof, dominates this end of Colmore Row. The dining room of the Great Western Hotel was converted to an emergency casualty post and itself was badly damaged in an air raid on the night of 20 November 1940. The two Birmingham Leyland 'Titan' TD6cs with Metro-Cammell bodies look a little careworn and still have their dark-painted camouflaged roofs. Both buses have just turned out of Livery Street and are loading up at the former tram shelters in their own carriageway. The leading EOG-registered bus is working on the 72 service to the Hawthorns. (D.R. Harvey Collection)

2189 (JOJ 189) was one of the first fifteen Leyland 'Titan' PD2/1s to be bodied by Park Royal with the front destination box fitted about 3in too high up. As a result the middle blue livery band was straight and lacked the normal dip below the box and the thinner livery centre section. After this error in complying with BCT's body specifications, it was another thirteen years before Park Royal were awarded another body building contract. This attractive-looking bus is working on the 72 service to the Hawthorns. Interestingly, the BCT bus inspector has strategically placed himself in the narrow roadway, thereby ensuring that the Leyland's bus driver doesn't leave the stop early. (A.J. Douglas)

One of the longest-lived Leyland-bodied 'Titan' PD2/1s was 2140 (JOJ 140), being withdrawn in December 1968. During the apparently never-ending run of the *Sound of Music* at the Gaumont Cinema, which had a 168-week run between 1965 and 1968, the bus swings around Colmore Circus, when working on the 75 route to Wednesbury. This was when the city terminus of the route was outside the still new *Birmingham Post & Mail* building, seen here in the background on the right. The Gaumont was officially opened on 9 February 1931 with the film *Raffles* starring Ronald Colman. (M. Fenton)

In July 1984, a seven-year-old Metro-Cammell-bodied Daimler 'Fleetline' FE30AGR speeds around the now gone 1963-built Colmore Circus. 6469 (NOC 469R) is working on the inbound 74 service from Dudley and West Bromwich. Over 1,800 West Midlands PTE 'Fleetlines' with this style of body were built by both Metro-Cammell and Park Royal, bought between July 1971 and May 1979, and were the stalwarts of the fleet until the last ones were withdrawn on 1 November 1997. (D.R. Harvey)

Travelling down Snow Hill in about 1905 is CBT Cable Car 116. This open-top bogie car was built by Metropolitan RCW in 1898 and seated twenty-four passengers outside and twenty longitudinally in the lower saloon. The central slot between the running rails is for the cable which was gripped by the tram in order for it to move. The second railway station at Snow Hill was still in use as the removal of the large single-span iron bridge only began in 1906, and one of the advertisements is a sign for the GWR and the Great Central Railway jointly operating at High Wycombe, which only started in 1905. (D.R. Harvey Collection)

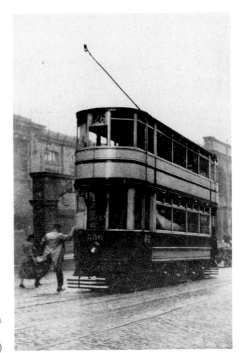

In about 1934, a man jumps on to a 26 route tram which is going to Oxhill Road, Handsworth. Car 530, a UEC-built bogie tram of 1913, was mounted on Mountain & Gibson Burnley-type maximum traction bogies. This meant that the large outer wheels carried up to 80 per cent of the trams 15¾ tons while the small wheels helped to stabilize the car. The tram is alongside the side goods entrance to Snow Hill Station's Platform 12. (Commercial Postcard)

Climbing up Snow Hill in about 1960 is 2801 (JOJ 801). This Crossley-bodied Daimler CVG6 entered service on 1 July 1952 in time for the Bristol Road tramway conversion. By now based at Harborne Garage, this bus is working on the cross-city 7 route to Portland Road, located within a mile of Cape Hill. The descent of Snow Hill was all the more noticeable from here because of the increasingly high wall of brickwork necessary to ensure the railway station's level formation across the distant Great Charles Street and the valley of the tiny Fleet Brook. Parked opposite the bus is a pre-war Opel Kadett. (A.J. Douglas)

Speeding down Snow Hill from the distant Boots the Chemists on the corner of Bull Street and
Colmore Row is this MCCW-bodied Daimler CVD6, 1801 (HOV 801), with an exposed radiator. This
bus is working on the 72 service to the city boundary at the Hawthorns in about 1960. Following the
bus is an almost new Bedford TK lorry, a model which had only been introduced that year. (A.J. Douglas)

Snow Hill Queensway came into being when the buildings on the eastern side were cleared away in
the early 1960s, leaving the old roadway of Snow Hill to be an access to the rapidly declining Snow
Hill Station. In about 1970, under West Midlands PTE ownership but still in its original West Bromwich
Corporation livery, 197H (PEA 197) turns out of Colmore Circus and into Snow Hill Queensway,
working on the 74 service to Dudley. This bus is a Daimler CVG6 with a Willowbrook H34/26R body
built in 1957. (D.R. Harvey)

In about 1965, looking freshly repainted, 2171 (JOJ 171), one of the fifty Leyland-bodied Leyland PD2/1s of 1949, quickly gathers speed as it travels down the recently completed Snow Hill Queensway. It is working on the Oxhill Road 70 service, which leaves the main Soho Road in the middle of Handsworth's shopping centre. To the left is Lloyd House, the West Midlands Police Headquarters. (A.D. Broughall)

The 79 service between Birmingham and Wolverhampton via Darlaston began operating on 28 February 1971. It was operated by Hockley, Oak Lane and Bilston Street garages, and while the Birmingham and West Bromwich garages used fifty-four to fifty-eight-seat buses, 187 (MDA 187E) was the first of the final batch of thirty-one 30ft-long Guy 'Arab' Vs delivered in 1967, but their lives were cut short when it was discovered at the time of their mid-life overhauls that their Strachan seventy-two-seat bodies were going to be too expensive to renovate. Because of their small Gardner 6LW engines they were underpowered, and outside their home town they were not popular because they were fitted with sliding doors. The bus, still in its Wolverhampton Corporation livery, is picking up passengers in Snow Hill Queensway, working on the 79 route on a foul day in 1971. Surprisingly, 187 would be one of just three of the class to be repainted in the WMPTE blue and cream livery. (L. Mason)

Looking from Slaney Street, nearly opposite Great Charles Street, up Snow Hill towards Colmore Row, the cable conduit and tram tracks are being laid in early 1888. Snow Hill Station's buildings are just visible beyond the wall of advertisements, while on the left are the mainly early Victorian buildings which were all converted to retail premises. The sheer labour intensity of undertaking this civil engineering project is staggering, not least because the main tools used were picks and shovels. (D.R. Harvey Collection)

Travelling up Snow Hill Queensway on 25 May 2002, travelling into Birmingham, is TWM 4164 (Y762 TOH). This Dennis 'Trident' with an Alexander H47/28F body entered service in June 2001. It is working on the 79 service from Wolverhampton. On the right is the 1960s-built Lloyd House which is the Headquarters of West Midland Police and behind the bus is the tall 133-room Thistle Hotel on the corner of the distant St Chad's Queensway. (D.R. Harvey)

2

CONSTITUTION HILL
TO HOCKLEY

Speeding down Constitution Hill on a cross-city 15 service from Hamstead to Whittington Oval in Yardley is 2448 (JOJ 448). This bus is travelling from Hockley towards the city centre in about 1966. This 'new look'-fronted Crossley DD42/6 has a Crossley H30/24R body, and has just passed the entrance to Summer Lane on the right and the impressive triangular, terracotta and red brick building built in 1896 known as the Red Palace. Looking like the prow of a ship, the premises were built as a memorial to Lord Roberts of Kandahar who became the commander-in-chief of the British Army during the Boer War. (D.R. Harvey Collection)

Overtaking the parked 1524 (GOE 524), a 1947 MCCW H30/24R-bodied Daimler CVA6 working on the peak-hours-only 25 route is 2666 (JOJ 666). This 1951 'new look'-fronted Daimler CVD6 with a Metro-Cammell body is travelling down Constitution Hill on the 72 service from the city boundary at the Hawthorns. The bus still has a full set of chrome radiator trims and full-length front wings. On the right is the chemical and electro-plating factory of W. Canning. 2666 has one of the experimental sealed radiator systems identifiable by the box above the front lower saloon window. (A.D. Broughall)

By 2007 Cannings had long since disappeared, but their former premises dating from the 1950s survived as small industrial units. On 25 April 2007, travelling out of the city centre up Constitution Hill on the 79 service is 4606 (BX 54 DDU), a Dennis 'Trident' 338 BR with an Alexander H45/28F, which entered service in October 2004. Since their delivery, these excellent Wolverhampton-based buses have been the mainstay of both the 79 and 126 services between Birmingham and Wolverhampton. (D.R. Harvey)

1768 (HOV 768) was one of fourteen Metro-Cammell-bodied Daimler CVD6s allocated to Hockley Garage. On 27 April 1962, the bus is crossing Constitution Hill having come out of Great Hampton Row, working on the 69 service from Lozells. It is about to turn into Livery Street and return to the terminus alongside Snow Hill Station. The elaborately styled late 1890s building behind the bus on the corner of Great Hampton Row and Great Hampton Street was originally built for the Royal Liver Friendly Society, but the ground floor was occupied by the appropriately named Gothic Inn public house, which closed in 1991. (D.F. Potter)

A Brush totally enclosed bogie, Car 620, dating from the end of 1920, has just crossed the outbound tracks in Great Hampton Street as it starts its turn into Livery Street as it nears the end of its 9-mile journey from Wednesbury, working on the 75 service on Sunday 26 March 1939. The tram has just passed the electro-plating and chemicals factory of W. Canning on the far corner of Kenyon Street, only one week before the abandonment of Handsworth trams. (L. W. Perkins)

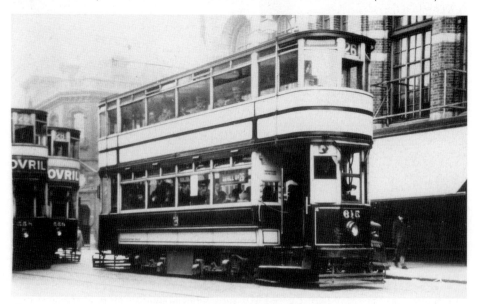

Great Hampton Street took the Soho Road trams along a road lined with metal spinners, brass founders, capstan lathe operators and sundry business involved in the jewellery trade. Brush-built and totally enclosed, this bogie Car 615 travels along Great Hampton Street when working on the 26 route from Oxhill Road on 28 March 1939. Behind the tram is Barclays Bank on the corner of Great King Street, which is partially masked by the slightly older UEC-built trams 558 and 559. (L. W. Perkins)

One of the bus routes running through Hockley is the 16 service to Hamstead. After bus de-regulation in October 1986, Birmingham Coach Co. became the first independent operator to register a service in competition with Travel West Midlands. Re-named Diamond Bus in 2000, the operator now employs a fleet of modern single-deckers. On 13 February 2008 bus 207 (YG 51 EKG), a fairly uncommon VDL bus DE02 with a Wright B39F body which entered service in September 2001, travels along Great Hampton Street, passing the art nouveau brick-fronted Crowngate Apartments, built in the 1880s for Midland Bank. (D.R. Harvey)

1803 (HOV 803), a Daimler CVD6 with a Metro-Cammell H30/24R body, entered service as a normal member of the 1756–1843 class on 1 July 1948, but after just one year it re-entered service with the proposed triple-indicator destination boxes that would be used on the 'new look'-fronted buses due to enter service in 1950. The bus is travelling through the busy junction at Hockley Brook and will shortly begin the steep climb up Hockley Hill on its way into Birmingham in about 1961. The Daimler CVD6s were powered by a Daimler CD6 8.6-litre engine which ran very quietly but consumed a good deal of engine oil. As a result these early post-war Daimler-engined buses were withdrawn without reaching old age. (F.W. York)

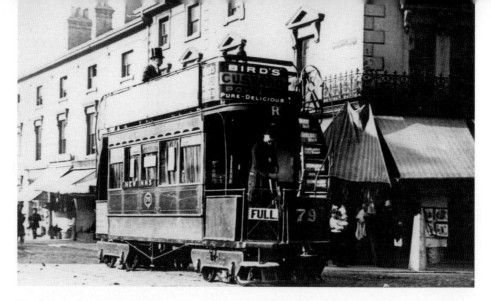

The Birmingham Central Tramways Co. opened its cable tram service as far as Hockley Brook on 24 March 1888, where the first continuous cable from Colmore Row ended. The outer section of the route to the New Inns, Handsworth, using the second cable, was opened on 20 April 1889. Waiting at the junction with Farm Street, opposite Whitmore Street where the depot was sited, is bogie Cable Car 79. This was one of the original 1888 open-toppers built by Falcon. The tram is standing outside the Cable Tramway Inn just beyond the gap between the two cables, and the tram driver is moving the cable-gripper levers in order to get the tram underway to Birmingham. (Newman College)

The mid-nineteenth-century buildings on the north-eastern side of Hockley Brook still remained on Friday 31 March 1939. Cars 548 and 534 have come down Soho Hill on their way in to the city. Car 548 has come in from Oxhill Road on the 26 route while 534 is on the 28 route from the New Inns at Handsworth. The leading tram is about to overtake a Smethwick-registered Standard Flying Ten. The tram tracks turning to the left lead into Whitmore Street, thereby giving access to Hockley Depot. (H.B. Priestley)

About to turn right into Whitmore Street, with the driver hanging his hand out of the cab door window prior to making his traffic signal, is 1120 (CVP 220). The bus is returning from the Hawthorns on a shortworking back to Hockley. This bus had an unusual history. It is a Daimler COG5, and entered service on 4 November 1937, but during the post-war body changes, 1120 acquired an English Electric H28/26R body in February 1949. This was one of twenty 'streamline'-bodied buses intended for Manchester Corporation and was purchased initially to re-body some of the vehicles whose bodies were destroyed when Hockley Garage was bombed in November 1940. Behind the bus is the old Tramway Inn building and the later gable-ended retail premises at the bottom of Soho Hill. (D.R. Harvey Collection)

Bought in 1892, 'The Julian' was an EEC battery locomotive which was bought by Birmingham Central tramways to tow the cable trams from Hockley Depot along Whitmore Street to Hockley Brook so that they could be attached to one of the two cables. The loco is standing on the forecourt in front of the still fairly new Hockley Depot and is attached to Cable Car 90. This was a Falcon open-top bogie car which sat twenty-four outside and twenty in the lower saloon, built in 1888 for the opening of the cable system. (D.R. Harvey Collection)

Parked at the entrance to rows 1 to 4 are four of the standard bogie cars allocated to Hockley Depot. Staff from the depot take the opportunity to pose in front of the row of tramcars on 29 March 1939, three days before the Soho Road routes were abandoned. Trams 542, 516 and 552 are all pre-First World War UEC-built trams mounted on M&G Burnley-bogies. Cars 542 and 552 were re-motored with 63hp motors between 1925 and 1927 while 516 received a 70hp motor at the same time. The odd tram out is Car 635 which was built by Brush in 1921 and again re-motored in the late 1920s with a 63hp motor. By the time the trams were abandoned in 1939, Hockley Depot had an allocation of 110 trams. (W.A. Camwell)

The tramcar used to close the Soho Road routes to West Bromwich and Dudley was ex-Radial-truck Car 128. It nominally operated as a 73 service starting in Carter's Green. Car 551 was the last tram to Wednesbury, and on its return to Carter's Green its passengers were transferred to the elderly Car 128. Meanwhile 551 returned to Dudley and in darkness went to Selly Oak Depot via the West Smethwick route. This was one of the twenty-one Hockley bogie cars which went back to their new depots via 'the Track'. Car 128 is travelling along Whitmore Street in its final moments of glory as by the time it returned to Hockley Depot in the early hours of Sunday 2 April 1939 it had been stripped of nearly every unscrewable souvenir. Not surprisingly, 128 was taken to West Smethwick Depot where Cashmores broke it up two months later. (D.R. Harvey Collection)

The conversion of the Soho Road tram routes to bus operation, with the cross-boundary bus services to Wednesbury and Dudley jointly operated with West Bromwich Corporation, went remarkably smoothly. Within twenty months of this harmonious change-over, operations were disastrously affected on the night of 19 November 1940 when Hockley Garage received a huge direct hit in a heavy air raid. The tangled mass of body frames were cleared quickly and although twenty-three bodies were burnt out, by 1942 all had been either re-bodied with English Electric bodies intended for Manchester Corporation or received rebuilt units. Amazingly, only six almost new buses were totally destroyed. (BCT)

Parked alongside the Whitmore Street Garage yard wall is Metro-Cammell-bodied Leyland 'Titan' TD6c 212 (EOG 212). The whole class of eighty-five buses were allocated to Hockley Garage for the extensive overnight conversion of the Birmingham Corporation tram routes along Soho Road and beyond to West Bromwich, Wednesbury and Dudley on 2 April 1939. These Leylands had torque converter gearboxes which were the predecessors of automatic gearboxes in modern-day buses. While being easy to drive because of their lack of clutch pedal, their fuel consumption was very poor. Their engine speed always seemed to be at odds with the road speed, and they whirred away until they got to about 20mph when the driver pulled back the gear lever from the torque position and put the bus into 'Drive'. (A.D. Broughall)

BCT ordered ten rear-engined Leyland 'Atlantean' PDR1/1 chassis which were delivered from Lancashire in the early part of 1961. They were all stored on the Whitmore Street side of Hockley Garage until Metro-Cammell was able to take them over for bodying at their Elmdon Factory. The buses, numbered 3231–3240 (231–240 DOC), all entered service on 5 November 1961, with the first five being allocated to Hockley Garage in order to convert the short 96 service to large-capacity vehicles. The former CBT cable car depot became a Corporation tram depot, survived being bombed and became one of West Midland PTE's garages, but despite being the oldest premises in the Travel West Midlands operating area, the garage was closed in May 2005. (L. Mason)

In the post-war years Hockley Garage had an allocation of usually between two and four of the Weymann-bodied Leyland 'Tiger' PS2/1 single-deckers. These were not usually used in public service, but were employed on school services. 2231 (JOJ 231), the first of these thirty elegant vehicles, was still fairly new when it was used by these three drivers to pose alongside in about 1956. These were the only post-war Birmingham buses to have a recessed windscreen and an exposed radiator. Buses 2231–2236 were the only ones of the batch to have their side destination boxes mounted above the first bay, as later buses were constructed with the box positioned over the second bay. 2231 has been preserved since 1971. (D.R. Harvey)

The Inner Circle 8 route crosses Hockley Brook and from the easterly direction used Hunter's Road to traverse the main A41 road. On 15 July 2004 the author's preserved 1950 bus, 2489 (JOJ 489), a Crossley DD42/6 with a Crossley H30/24R body, stands where the Bundy Clock used to be located as it operates on a demonstration service around the route. Behind the bus is the former jewellery manufacturing premises of H. Samuel's. The historical significance of this bus is that it was one of the class of 100 Crossleys fitted with the 'new look' concealed radiator. It was so called because the wide-hipped bonnet cowl tapered down towards the ground in a way reminiscent of Christian Dior's early post-war 'new look' dress designs. Well, that was the theory! (D.R. Harvey)

For nearly nineteen years the mainstays of Hockley Garage's bus fleet were the fifty Leyland-bodied 'Titan' PD2/1s. 2162 (JOJ 162) entered service on 1 May 1949 and, unusually, was withdrawn on Leap Year Day, 1968, by which time it had run nearly 470,000 miles. The bus is passing through Hockley Brook, having descended Soho Hill, working on the 72 route from the Handsworth boundary at the Hawthorns. The bus is at the stop opposite Whitmore Street where Hockley Garage was located in about 1958. The large three-storey shops behind the bus were part of Hockley's important late Victorian shopping centre, including the Birmingham Municipal Bank on the corner of Farm Street. (R.H.G. Simpson)

Six months after the Leyland-bodied Leyland PD2/1s were delivered to Hockley, the garage received the fifteen new buses from the next class of buses. These too were Leyland 'Titan' PD2/1s but had attractive Park Royal H29/25R bodies. 2190 (JOJ 190) was one of these fifteen buses which also had a straight blue middle livery band because the bodybuilder had fitted the front destination box too high up the front panel. In service the bus averaged about 2,000 miles a month and totalled 462,537 miles by the time it was withdrawn on 31 May 1969. 2190 is at the Farm Street junction in Hockley Brook in 1958, travelling to Birmingham on the 72 service. (R.H.G. Simpson)

Hockley fly-over was opened in early 1968 and by December of the same year 2131 (JOJ 131) was withdrawn from service. This is the first of fifty Leyland-bodied Leyland PD2/1s of 1949 which would spend almost all of their operational lives at Hockley Garage. The bus is going back to the garage having come probably from the city boundary at the Hawthorns. The garage entrance at this time lay behind the distant row of bus shelters on the far side of Soho Hill (G. Yates)

The passenger shelters on Soho Hill for the outbound trams were sited in a somewhat strange position, being in the middle of the wide entrance to Claremont Road. UEC-built bogie Car 544 is picking up passengers on the 26 service to Oxhill Road. The tram is carrying a balcony-dash panel for the *Evening Despatch*, a local newspaper which was published between 1902 and 1963. (R. T. Wilson)

Birmingham's first Leyland 'Atlantean' PDR1/1 was a Leyland demonstrator registered 460 MTE, which entered service at Lea Hall Garage in February 1960. After being re-engined with the larger 0.680 11.1-litre 'Power Plus' unit, the bus was purchased in May 1961 and given the fleet number 3230. The bus remained at Lea Hall until November 1961 when it joined the first five of the Leyland 'Atlanteans' purchased for comparison with the similarly rear-engined Daimler 'Fleetlines'. The bus was normally employed on the 96 Lodge Road service, but occasionally it was let out onto the 'mainline'. 3230 is travelling down Soho Hill on the 72 route from Handsworth. (D.R. Harvey Collection)

Climbing up Soho Hill during the start of the construction of Hockley flyover is 2182 (JOJ 182). This was the second of the Park Royal-bodied Leyland 'Titan' PD2/1s and was one of only sixteen of the fifty buses of this type to have entered service in 1949. It is working on the 75 route to Wednesbury and is negotiating the barriers and fencing opposite the junction with Hamstead Road. 2182 is being followed by a Mini, an almost new Vauxhall Victor VX4/90 and a Volkswagen 'splitty' Microbus. (R.H.G. Simpson)

In about 1904, a CBT cable car climbs Soho Hill. Having left Hockley Brook on the second continuous cable, the tram is on its way to the New Inns at Handsworth. The west side of the main road is occupied by early nineteenth-century houses while dominating the east side of Soho Hill is the rather ungainly tower built on top of Soho Hill Congregational Chapel. On the right, with the decorative brickwork, is the gilt jewellery and stud manufacturer Sydney Griffith. (Commercial Postcard)

3

HANDSWORTH TO
THE BOUNDARY

A horse-drawn wagon pulls out of Villa Road behind a cable car travelling into Soho Hill. The cable car is passing the Old Gate Glass and China Repository, dated from the 1880s, which is still there as a retail outlet at the time of writing. CBT Car 176 was one of six built in 1902 by the company as an open-top forty-four-seat bogie car. It would appear that at this time CBT was content to continue operating the cable car route from Colmore Row to the New Inns when they bought this final batch of trams, but on 8 October 1909 Handsworth UDC bought the line from Hockley Brook to the New Inns. As the city had resolved to electrify their inner section when the lease expired on 30 June 1911, this spelled the end for the cable car system, leaving Car 176 to be scrapped after only nine years of life. (Commercial Postcard)

Standing at the western terminus of the 5 route from Gravelly Hill is UEC four-wheel open-balcony Car 373. The tram is in Villa Road on 1 October 1938 and is parked just short of the junction with Soho Road. There had been a proposal by the Corporation to link the Soho Road and Villa Road services when the electrification of the mainline route took place on 1 July 1911. This was never constructed, so the distant enclosed bogie car in Soho Road always trundled past Villa Road with the gap of about 50 yards never being connected. Thus the idea of being able to go from the Hawthorns to Villa Park by tram never materialised. (W.A. Camwell)

Above: The Guru Nanak Sikh Gurdwara, named after the founding father of Sikhism, stands at the 'gateway' to the Soho Road shopping centre. The impressive temple is located on the corner of Rose Hill Road and Soho Road and is diagonally opposite the Grade II listed St Michael's Church dating from 1855. On 30 March 2004, 4547 (BL 53 EEG), a Travel West Midlands Transbus 'Trident' SFD334 with an Alexander H47/28F body, has just reached the traffic lights opposite Villa Road, working on the 79 route outward from Birmingham. (D.R. Harvey)

Right: Seen on Soho Road, Handsworth, just beyond Waverhill Road travelling away from Hockley, is Brush-built bogie Car 611. The tram entered service during the summer of 1920 with enclosed vestibules and open balconies and a seating capacity of sixty-two. As the balconies of all the 587-636 class were enclosed by November 1931, Car 611 would have been working on the 26 service to Oxhill Road prior to these enclosures. On the right are some of the late nineteenth-century retail premises, which are still trading in the early twenty-first century. (W.H. Bett)

The foundation stone of Handsworth Council House was laid on 30 October 1877 on the former site of an old inn called the Waggon & Horses, and represented Handsworth's civic pride and fierce independence from nearby Birmingham. The impressive Handsworth Council House was designed by A.E. Henman and built in red brick and terracotta with stone dressings and a slate roof. The two-storey building has a steeply pitched roof and an impressive clock tower. It was opened by 1879 as the Urban District's Council Offices. Ten years later the second half of the CBT cable tram route was opened from Hockley to the New Inns. Car 89, built by the Falcon Co. of Loughborough in 1888 as an open-top bogie double-decker, travels past the Council House through the already developing shopping centre in Soho Road towards Hockley, around the end of the Victorian era. (Commercial Postcard)

BCT Tram 357 loads up with a large number of passengers at the corner of Stafford Road outside the Frighted Horse public house which at this time, before the First World War, was selling Cheshire's Windmill Ales. Some of these four-wheel UEC-bodied trams were initially allocated to Hockley Depot when new, but were replaced when the larger 512-class bogie cars were delivered in 1914. This stop was a terminal point for a short working on the Soho Road route and was later given the route number 27. The tramcar in front of 357 is South Staffordshire Black Country Through Car 41, which is outside the imposing Handsworth Council House, and has just passed the outbound BCT Tram 284. (Commercial Postcard)

In about 1926, the almost new Brush-bodied Brush Burnley bogie Car 625, still with open balconies, travels along Soho Road through the busy shopping centre. It is working on the 74 service to Dudley, and has just passed the junction with Holliday Road and is almost opposite the former Handsworth Council House. Behind the approaching Maudslay Subsidy lorry, still running on rubber tyres, is the Elite Cinema which was opened on 30 September 1913, making it quite an early suburban cinema. (Commercial Postcard)

Approaching Ninevah Road in August 1994 in Soho Road is West Midland Travels 2048 (BOK 48V). This MCW 'Metrobus' DR102/12 Mk I with a H43/30F seating layout entered service in March 1980 and is working on the 78 route to Wolverhampton. These buses were the backbone of both the WMPTE and Travel fleets from 1978 until 2001, being the largest fleet of the model to be operated outside London. 2048 had been recently repainted in the blue and silver livery with a broad red stripe which looked good when fresh but weathered badly. (D.R. Harvey)

The last of the fifty Leyland-bodied Leyland 'Titan' PD2/1s of 1949 was 2180 (JOJ 180). It entered service on 1 June 1949 and had a long working life of just over nineteen years. It is at the inbound bus stop just beyond the Grove Lane junction where Dudley's furniture store was located. 2180 is working on the 72 route from the Handsworth boundary. Alongside the bus and behind the utility bus shelter is the local Sketchley dry cleaners shop which had been for many years a gas showroom. Just above the bus is a long-redundant tramway traction pole with its decorative finial on the top. (D.R. Harvey)

The turn into Grove Lane, guarded by a branch of the Birmingham Municipal Bank and Dudley's furniture store on the left, took the Oxhill Road 26 route away from Soho Road. Passing the junction on its way back to Birmingham on 25 March 1939 is Car 540, an eight-wheeled bogie, working on the 23 service from the city boundary at the Hawthorns, while travelling out of the city is the similar UEC-bodied Car 546. The driver of the small lorry passing over the Belisha crossing is apparently oblivious to the pedestrians walking across Soho Road. (D. Clayton)

The Oxhill Road service was opened on 20 November 1912. Car 614 has turned right from Soho Road into Grove Lane, working on the 26 route in about 1934. It is travelling towards Soho Road, having just passed the junction in Dawson Road. This Brush-built totally enclosed bogie tram is passing the impressive buildings of Handsworth Grammar School for Boys, founded in August 1862. (Commercial Postcard)

GROVE LANE, HANDSWORTH. (41)

The Oxhill Road tram route terminated at the shops behind the tramcar on the corner of Stockwell Road. Opposite the tram is Rookery Road, traversed by the Outer Circle 11 bus route. BCT had applied to extend the 26 tram route along Rookery Road and back to Soho Road, forming what would have been a very useful loop around Handsworth, but although powers were obtained nothing was ever built. Car 608, a Brush-bodied bogie, waits at the terminus on 25 March 1939 before beginning the 3½-mile journey back to the city centre. (A.N.H. Glover)

The 70 bus service was the replacement for the 26 tram route and began operation on 2 April 1939. The route was extended by about ½ mile from the tram terminus at Rookery Road to the bottom of Island Road at the Uplands public house. The Uplands was opened on 16 September 1932 and after trading for nearly eighty years it was demolished in 2009. 2229 (JOJ 229), a Leyland 'Titan' PD2/1 with a Park Royal H29/25R body, waits at the Bundy Clock outside the pub in about 1964. 2229 ultimately became the only exposed radiator BCT bus to operate for WMPTE, and was withdrawn on 30 November 1969. Even then its career was not quite over as it was cut down to a towing vehicle by Wombwell Diesels, finally being used to tow away the last of Walsall's trolleybuses from Birchills Garage. (D. Johnson)

Looking from Soho Road post office, on the left, with the tower of the Midland Bank next door on the corner of Baker Street, towards Grove Lane where a white-coated policeman strikes a lonely figure on point duty, Handsworth's main arterial road is apparently not very busy. On this sunny day when many of the shops have their canvas blinds extended, an early 1934 Austin Seven travels towards the New Inns while in the distance tramcar 596 awaits instructions from the lonesome policeman at the Grove Lane junction. (Commercial Postcard)

Turning out of Boulton Road into the main shopping centre of Handsworth in Soho Road is 1755 (HOV 755). This was one of Perry Barr Garage's allocations of 1948-vintage Leyland 'Titan' PD2/1s with Brush H30/24R bodywork, and belonged to a class of buses that were normally not seen on the main Soho Road services, though they were regular performers on the Outer Circle route. The well-laden 1755 is working on an Outer Circle 'shortworking' back to Perry Barr in about 1965. (R.H.G. Simpson)

Picking up a long queue of passengers outside the Red Lion public house in Soho Road is AEA 14. Numbered 84 in the West Bromwich Corporation fleet, this Daimler COG6 was fitted with a Metro-Cammell H30/26R body and is working on the 74 service. This body style was developed for Edinburgh Corporation and is subtly different from the pre-war BCT equivalent as it did not have the Birmingham-style straight staircase. The Red Lion, positioned directly opposite the Boulton Road junction, was built as a Holts Brewery house in 1902 in plum-coloured terracotta brickwork with Flemish tracery and a vaguely Jacobean look to its storeys. Previously there was a hostelry on this site in Soho Road from 1829. (C. Carter)

One of the best ideas of Travel West Midlands was to repaint a number of their buses in the liveries of the original constituent municipalities. Looking absolutely splendid in West Bromwich Corporation's livery of yellow with lined-out dark and light blue panelling is 3033 (F33 XOF). This Mk II MCW 'Metrobus' is travelling out of the city on Soho Road and is about to pass the junction with Alfred Road. The row of shops to the left of the bus was originally built for the Birmingham Co-op in 1914, but on 19 March 1996, when visited by the author, was occupied by a variety of Asian sweet centres and a supermarket. (D.R. Harvey)

The Regal Cinema on the corner of Booth Street was the largest suburban cinema in Birmingham with seating for 2,150 people. It was designed by Harold Seymour Scott who designed seven other picture houses in the suburbs of the city and was opened on 13 October 1928. The Regal's other claim to fame was that it was the first cinema in Birmingham to be equipped for the new 'Talkies'. Car 602, built in 1920 by Brush, passes the cinema in about 1934 as it nears its terminus at the New Inns, working on the 28 route. (Commercial Postcard)

When the Handsworth tram route was taken over by Birmingham Corporation on 1 July 1911, the trams used were members of the 221-class of open-top tramcars built by UEC on Brill 21E 6ft wheelbase trucks. These trams were operated from the Miller Street Depot until June 1912 when the conversion of Hockley Depot from cable to electric tram operation was completed. Travelling down Holyhead Road from the New Inns is Car 236 which entered service during April 1907. Seen here soon after the takeover in the late summer of 1911; as if the tram hasn't got enough to negotiate on the road surface, it is having to use the old cable car tracks, while the sagging overhead is a most unusual feature for tramcar operations by BCT! (D.R. Harvey Collection)

Approaching the New Inns in Holyhead Road and climbing up the gentle slope from Booth Street in about 1974 is Park Royal-bodied Daimler 'Fleetline' CRG6LX 4089 (YOX 89K). This bus entered service in September 1971 and remained in operation until 1984. The bus is working on the 74E route which, although showing Dudley as its destination, is probably only going as far as West Bromwich. (D.R. Harvey)

One of the last batch of cable cars delivered to CBT in 1902 was open-top bogie Tram 177. This open-top forty-four-seat cable car was built at Kyotts Road Works by CBT. It is travelling away from the distant Booth Street junction on Holyhead Road in about 1905 and is passing the Ashbury Memorial Chapel located on the corner of Milestone Lane, whose spire towers over the surrounding houses. The chapel was named after Francis Ashbury, who was born in Newton Road in the late eighteenth century to become a founder of the Methodist Episcopal Church of America. It is noticeable that the quality of the houses on the right are distinctly inferior to the villas set in their own grounds on the left. (Commercial Postcard)

The terminus of the CBT cable cars was the New Inns, Handsworth, on the corner of Sandwell Road and Crocketts Lane. The second half of the route was opened from Hockley on 20 April 1889. Although neither of the two cable cars is identifiable, the one on the right is one of the original 1888 Falcon-built trams while the tram on the left is a 1902-vintage CBT-built tram. The New Inns, a Mitchells & Butlers-owned public house, in this form, was not opened until 1901 when it replaced a much older inn. The brewery extended the property in 1904 when the Assembly Rooms were opened, which are on the right of the cable tram. The interior of the New Inns was decorated with art nouveau ceramic tiles and its opulence made it a prime venue for weddings and other important functions. Throughout the 1980s it remained derelict, but most of the building was eventually saved and converted into flats by November 1995. In the distance on the other side of Crocketts Road are two South Staffordshire open-top electric bogie trams. (Commercial Postcard)

South Staffordshire Tividale-built Car 62 leaves the New Inns, behind the trees on the right, on the Black Country Through Service from Darlaston to Birmingham. It is travelling towards Colmore Row on a section of tram track which is in dire need of replacement. This tram was one of the first trams built by B&M to have enclosed platforms with permanent protection for the driver. This was one of two cars of this type which entered service with South Staffordshire in early 1916. (D.R. Harvey Collection)

Picking up passengers in Holyhead Road is this rebuilt UEC-built totally enclosed M&G Burnley-bogied Tram 559. It is waiting outside Lloyds Bank in early 1939, just short of the New Inns on the distant corner of Crocketts Lane. The tram is working on the 28 route which terminated at the cross-over at the New Inns and was the successor to the old CBT cable-car terminus. (R.T. Wilson)

Travelling down Holyhead Road towards the New Inns, working on the 72 route from the Birmingham-West Bromwich boundary at the Hawthorns, is 1297 (FOF 297). This class of fifty buses were some of the most attractive Birmingham buses ever to be built, combining the elegance of the last pre-war style of Colin Bailey-designed Leyland bodies with the detailed specification of Birmingham City Transport which included a straight staircase and BCT-style driver's door signalling windows. 1297, a Leyland 'Titan' TD6c with a fifty-two-seat Leyland body, was withdrawn on New Year's Eve 1953 having entered service some fourteen years earlier. (S.N.J. White)

At the Hawthorns, the Albion Depot was opened for electric trams on 20 December 1902 by the South Staffordshire Tramways Co., having originally been built in the 1880s as a steam tram depot. By 1906 it was only used as a parking space for up to eight trams when West Bromwich Albion was playing at home. After the 1924 takeover of the Dudley and Wednesbury tram services by BCT, the depot was still used on Saturday afternoons to park tramcars away from the already congested Holyhead Road. Totally enclosed bogie Cars 550, 613 and 616, the latter destined to carry the Civic Dignitaries on 4 July 1953 when it became Birmingham's Last Tram, wait with their assembled drivers and conductors at the depot in September 1939. After the Albion Depot was closed on 2 April 1939 it became industrial premises, but amazingly it was reconstructed at the Black Country Living Museum in Dudley as their tram depot. (W.A. Camwell)

Still looking in fine fettle after eleven years of arduous service, 229 (EOG 229), one of the eighty-five Leyland 'Titan' TD6cs with Metro-Cammell H28/24R bodywork bought for the tram replacement of April 1939, stands at the turning circle opposite the Hawthorns football ground on 8 October 1950. The bus is waiting to return to Birmingham on the 72 route short working, and only went to the city boundary at the Woodman public house. (G.F. Douglas, courtesy of A.D. Packer)

4

FOOTBALL SPECIALS TO WEST BROMWICH AND CARTER'S GREEN

On a rainy match day the supporters begin to stream away from the ground in order to catch trams heading for Handsworth and Birmingham. Apparently being ignored is Car 631, a Brush-bodied totally enclosed bogie, which is standing outside the M&B-owned Woodman public house in Holyhead Road facing West Bromwich in the shadow of the Hawthorns, the home of West Bromwich Albion FC. The tram is working on the 73 short working to Carter's Green. (J.S. Webb)

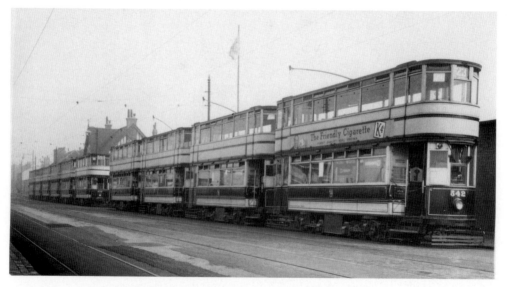

On Saturday 1 April 1939 the 'Baggies' reserves were playing at home, but, despite the comparative unimportance of the match, no less than ten eight-wheeled trams are waiting alongside the Hawthorns in Birmingham Road with the Woodman public house in the background. The rest of the first group of trams are 514, 517 and 636. The leading tram of the second group is Car 616 which was destined to become Birmingham's last tram on 4 July 1953. The leading tram, Brush Burnley bogie Car 542, had its balconies enclosed in December 1926 and was re-seated in April 1932 to be a sixty-one-seater. (L.W. Perkins)

1309 (FOF 309) was one of the buses purchased for the early wartime Dudley Road tram conversion scheme. This Leyland-bodied Leyland 'Titan' TD6c entered service on 1 October 1939 from Hockley Garage, but, after the closure of the Ladywood trams on 31 August 1947, all of this class were transferred to Rosebery Street. So when the bus was parked alongside the Hawthorns on a football special it was returning to its old haunts. Clearly visible is the tall torque converter gearbox header tank mounted just below the lower saloon front bulkhead window. This was filled with a mixture of oil and paraffin, which lubricated this simple to operate but expensive to maintain Lysholm Smith gearbox. (D.R. Harvey)

It is obviously match day at the 'Baggies' as hoards of fans make their way to the Hawthorns for the ensuing match. The bus is 2170 (JOJ 170), a Leyland-bodied Leyland 'Titan' PD2/1, built in 1949, which is unloading more football fans almost opposite Halford's Lane. Behind the bus is the stone wall bounding Sandwell Park. 2170 is working on the 75 route from Wednesbury towards Birmingham and is about two years old. (S.N.J. White)

When the 'Baggies' played at home, the queue of waiting buses standing alongside the Hawthorns started well before the Woodman public house and seemingly disappeared along Holyhead Road towards Halford's Lane, well beyond the football ground. In about 1952, as there are just two of that year's Weymann-bodied Daimler CVG6s in the line of buses, most of the buses are Daimler COG6s with MCCW bodies. Parked at the back of the row of buses is West Bromwich's solitary AEC 'Regent' 0661. By the late 1930s this marque was a rarity in the West Midlands. Even more unusually, this bus, 70 (EA 9064), was fitted with a rather elegantly styled Roe body. Behind this bus is an Austin A40 four-door Devon saloon registered during 1949 in Plymouth. (D. Williams)

A well-laden West Bromwich Corporation bus, 186 (KEA 186), a 1955 Daimler CVG6 fitted with a Metro-Cammell H32/26R body, pulls away from the bus shelter outside the Woodman public house. The bus is working towards Wednesbury on the 75 route. This pub, only demolished in 2004, not only marked the Birmingham West Bromwich boundary on Holyhead Road, but stood next to the Birmingham-end stand of the Hawthorns, home of West Bromwich Albion. This football ground is 547ft above sea level, surprisingly perhaps making it the highest football league ground in either England or Scotland. (R.H.G. Simpson)

Travelling across the Sandwell Valley along Birmingham Road towards West Bromwich is SOS
FEDD 2339 (FHA 843), a Brush-bodied forward entrance bus of 1939. The bus is working on the
220 route between Bearwood and Dartmouth Square, a bus service which was jointly operated
by Midland Red and West Bromwich Corporation. It has just turned left out of Halford's Lane
alongside the Hawthorns football ground, and is passing the impressive wall of Sandwell Park. This
had been the boundary for the Earl of Dartmouth's Sandwell Hall which dated from 1712 but was
demolished in 1928 due to mining subsidence. (A.B. Cross)

Speeding across the Sandwell Valley in early post-war years is 284 (EOG 284). This Metro-Cammell-
bodied Leyland 'Titan' TD6c is working on the 74 route in about 1946 and is still wearing the
khaki-camouflaged roof from the war. In addition the bus does look a little care worn with the
nearside front wing in particular looking rather battered. 284 would be one of the first of its class to
be taken out of service on 31 January 1950. (D.R. Harvey Collection)

Having crossed the Sandwell Valley, Birmingham Road became High Street at the eastern end of West Bromwich. Large gabled villas and terraces were built in the 1880s as part of the development of the town which was encouraged to some extent by the opening of Handsworth, Wednesbury and Darlaston steam tram service, operated by South Staffordshire & Birmingham District Steam Tramways Co., on 16 July 1883. Beyer Peacock Steam Loco 3, built in that year, hauls a sixty-seat Starbuck double-deck trailer (18) and is about to pass Bagnall Street in about 1900. (D.R. Harvey Collection)

About to cross from Birmingham Road into High Street is this well-laden BCT bus working on the 75 Wednesbury service. 2162 (JOJ 162), a Leyland 'Titan' PD2/1 with a Leyland H30/26R body, entered service on 1 May 1949 and would operate for the whole of its operational life of nineteen years from Hockley Garage. They were well suited to the fast running on the West Bromwich services, having large, powerful 9.6-litre engines and yet weighing only 7 tons 10cwt 3qtrs. They were also about 3in lower than the standard Birmingham bus and therefore had no problems with low bridges such as that at Dudley Port. (R.H.G. Simpson)

Travelling along High Street away from Dartmouth Square on its way back towards Handsworth is Travel West Midlands 4053 (V53 MOA). This Volvo B7TL entered service in November 1999, has a Plaxton H45/28F body which was originally designed and built by Northern Counties prior to this Wigan-based bodybuilder being taken over by Plaxtons in 1995 and production stopped in Lancashire in January 2005. The bus is working on the 74 route on 24 February 2009. (D.R. Harvey)

The South Staffordshire Tramways (Lessee) Co. opened the first part of its electric tramway from the Woodman Inn at the Handsworth boundary to Carter's Green on 19 December 1902. The route was extended over the B&M tracks beyond Burnt Tree to Dudley Station on 30 May 1903. Judging by the crowds standing in High Street at the Dartmouth Square junction, this might be that first day of operation. Standing under the unusual centre pole wiring, replaced in about 1913 by span wires, is SS Car 15. This tram was built by Brush in 1902 and mounted on Brush maximum traction bogies with the small pony wheels mounted outwards. It had a seating capacity of thirty-four inside and thirty-six outside, which was reached by reverse stairs. (Commercial Postcard)

At almost the same spot as the South Staffordshire Tram 15, but about fifty-five years later, 2191 (JOJ 191), a handsome Leyland 'Titan' PD2/1 with a Park Royal body, passes through Dartmouth Square on High Street, West Bromwich, with the Bull's Head public house, dating from 1835, on the extreme right at the corner of High Street and Spon Lane. With the saloon windows steamed-up, the bus is splashing through a heavy downpour as it works on the 75 route to Wednesbury in about 1958. (D.R. Harvey)

Car 59 was built by Brush in 1902 for the Wolverhampton District Electric Tramway and was one of four of their 14–30 class to be transferred to South Staffordshire in 1915. This open-top seventy-seater had Brush bogies and after its transfer was equipped with temporary vestibule screens. It is passing through Dartmouth Square in about 1920, towards Handsworth, with the clock tower opposite the junction with Spon Lane having replaced the elaborate drinking fountain installed by Reuben Farley in 1885. These tramcars, being open-top, could get underneath the bridge at Dudley Port and therefore operated on the Handsworth to Dudley line until the route was taken over by BCT in 1924. (D.R. Harvey Collection)

One of the last of the 1939 Daimler COG6s to remain in service was 79 (AEA 9), surviving until 1962. It was one of four of the class that were rebuilt by the corporation in the mid-1950s with rubber mounted glazing and sliding saloon ventilators. It is passing through the 'Golden Mile', which was the main shopping centre of West Bromwich, on High Street. Behind the bus, which is travelling towards Birmingham on the 74 route, is the chemist, Timothy Whites, which is next door to the Freeman, Hardy and Willis shoe shop. On the corner of Scotland Passage is the art deco-styled gentlemen's outfitters owned by Montague Burton and beyond that a Woolworth's store which survived until 2008. (A.D. Broughall)

Pulling away from the bus railings outside Burton's tailor shop is 2135 (JOJ 135). This Leyland 'Titan' PD2/1 with a fifty-six-seater Leyland body is again working on the 74 route from Dudley to Birmingham in about 1960. When ordered in 1948 for delivery the next year, Leyland Motors offered a straight staircase for these buses, but because of the small additional cost this option was not taken up. By now the bus is fitted with flashing indicators instead of trafficators and has an advertisement for King Kole which is too deep for the cream panel, but still looks much as it did ten years earlier when it was new. (J. Fozard)

Just into West Midland PTE days and still painted in West Bromwich Corporation livery is 198 (PEA 198). This bus is a 1957 Daimler CVG6 with a Willowbrook H34/26R body, and is working on the 74 route again towards Birmingham. It is picking up passengers outside Marks & Spencers in the High Street. These were the first sixty-seater buses purchased by the undertaking, but were the only ones purchased from this manufacturer due to the quality of the bodywork. The Willowbrook body could be easily distinguished by the inset upper saloon front windows. (D.R. Harvey Collection)

Other West Bromwich Corporation bus services other than the 74 and 75 'mainline' routes used the High Street. One was the 16 route which had replaced the old Birmingham & Midland single-deck tram route to West Smethwick and Oldbury introduced on 19 November 1929 and used both Spon Lane and Bromford Lane. Standing opposite Woolworth's in the High Street in August 1969 is one of the rather handsome Weymann-bodied Daimler CVG6s which dated from 1952. (D.J. Little)

Towards the end of Birmingham City Transport's operation, in 1969, Hockley Garage received some of Quinton Garage's 26ft-long Guy 'Arab' III Specials with Metro-Cammell H30/24R bodies. These replaced the rapidly diminishing numbers of exposed radiator Leyland PD2/1s which by the latter part of 1968 were being taken out of service. 2549 (JOJ 549), despite apparently not being sure of which route it is operating, is on High Street, again almost opposite Woolworth's store, in early 1969. (D.R. Harvey Collection)

Going towards Handsworth and Birmingham is UEC-built Car 548, built in early 1914. The tram is working on the 75 service from Wednesbury, and even in about 1930 High Street in the centre of West Bromwich is quite congested. The car in the foreground is a Standard 14/28 four-door tourer dating from about 1926. On the left with the magnificent lantern over the main door is the Sandwell public house located on the corner of New Street. (Commercial Postcard)

Speeding along New Street towards the original bus station in West Bromwich on 15 February 1987 is Mk II MCW 'Metrobus' 2696 (A 696 UOE). This bus entered service in December 1983 and is being employed here on the 74 route back to Birmingham. It is passing that doyen of 1970s and '80s electrical discount warehouse chains, Comet, which on this particular day, true to form, is in the middle of yet another sale! (D.R. Harvey)

In February 2009 West Bromwich Garage received a batch of brand new Scania Omnibus K230UBs with Scania B43F bodies. These single-deckers were purchased to upgrade the 404 service from Blackheath, Oldbury and West Bromwich to Walsall by way of Stone Cross. This is the new West Bromwich Bus Station which replaced the old 1970s one located next to Queen's Square Shopping Centre. That site was redeveloped with the new controversial Public Art Gallery, opened in late 2008. 1852 (BX58 SXS) leaves the strange gyratory road system in the new bus station on 24 February 2009 when only a few days old. (D.R. Harvey)

Approaching the junction with St Michael's Street on High Street is one of the first buses delivered to West Midlands PTE. 4005 (TOC 5H), was a Daimler 'Fleetline' CRG6LX, but although it had a body of the sort ordered by West Bromwich Corporation it was an extra built by Northern Counties in order to replace a Park Royal-bodied bus that was diverted to Johannesburg, South Africa, as a demonstrator. This two-door eighty-seater entered service in June 1970 and is working on the 90 route with the 130ft-high tower of the distant Town Hall, dating from 1874, dominating the skyline. (A.J. Douglas)

Travelling along High Street in the centre of West Bromwich is Car 520, approaching Dartmouth Square. It is passing the Warwickshire Household furnishing shop. This totally enclosed Brush-built 70hp bogie tramcar dates originally from 1914 but had been much rebuilt in the 1920s. The tram has just reversed at the St Michael's Street terrace of shops just short of New Street where the wonderfully fronted Sandwell public house is located. In the distance is the large Kenrick & Jefferson printing works. (W.A. Camwell)

On a rainy Saturday in 1933, Car 533 is working on the 73 route from Carter's Green. It has just passed the junction with New Street, having passed the tall building half hidden in the mist belonging to Kenrick & Jefferson who were one of Britain's biggest manufacturers of greetings cards, calendars and general stationery. Behind the Wolseley Series II 18/80 car is West Bromwich's Daimler COG5, 64 (AEA 9001), one of the four experimental buses purchased in 1937. These four were trialled prior to purchasing a fleet of new buses as their share of the tram replacement bus fleet to be jointly operated with Birmingham City Transport. (D.R. Harvey Collection)

The late Victorian three-storey premises with distinctive three-pointed attic gables were located between St Michael's RC Church and Victoria Street. On the opposite side of the road is 4038 (XON 38J). This Daimler 'Fleetline' CRG6LX had a seventy-six-seat Park Royal body of a style specified by WMPTE as their standard type which, with minor alterations, was also constructed by Metro-Cammell until May 1979. 4038 entered service in July 1971 and is working on the 74 route towards West Bromwich town centre on 4 March 1976. (E.V. Trigg)

Travelling out of West Bromwich along High Street and approaching West Bromwich Town Hall, working on the 75 route to Wednesbury, is this former West Bromwich Corporation bus. 201 (SEA 201), a Daimler CVG6 with a Metro-Cammell H37/26R body which entered service in December 1957, had an early repaint into the Oxford Blue and cream, a livery which took no account of the body mouldings fitted to separate the old West Bromwich Corporation livery. Behind the bus are the offices of Kenrick & Jefferson's printing works. (A.J. Douglas)

Standing in front of the West Bromwich Building Society's headquarters at 374 High Street, which is almost opposite West Bromwich Town Hall, is one of Hockley Garage's quiet and sophisticated Daimler CVD6s. Still wearing its 'dustbin lid'-style wheel trims, 2682 (JOJ 682) is heading into West Bromwich town centre on the 74 service from Dudley and Carter's Green in about 1954. Behind the bus is a Standard Vanguard Phase I, a model which was in production from 1948 until 1952. (G. Burrows)

On 24 February 2009, almost fifty-five years later, a Diamond Bus Dennis 'Dart' with a Plaxton B37F body, 472 (R458 LGH), passed the West Bromwich Building Society's premises on High Street on its way into West Bromwich town centre, working on the 74 route from Dudley. The trees in the background are in the churchyard of the former Christ Church. This was consecrated in 1829 and became the town centre's principal church but was closed in 1975 and demolished some five years later after being damaged by fire. All that was left was the churchyard, giving the town today an attractive open space. (D.R. Harvey)

The trees in the churchyard of Christ Church dominate the north-eastern side of High Street. Travelling towards the distant Baptist Chapel on the corner of Dartmouth Street is 2673 (JOJ 673), a Metro-Cammell-bodied Daimler CVD6 which is working on the 75 route towards Carter's Green and Wednesbury. Approaching the parked Ford V8 Pilot is 3163 (MOF 163). This Daimler CVG6, fitted with a Crossley H30/25R body, is travelling into West Bromwich on the 74 service. (D. Williams)

A rare bus short working was the 76 route to Great Bridge. 2166 (JOJ 166), a Leyland-bodied Leyland 'Titan' PD2/1, speeds through Carter's Green and is being followed by a West Bromwich Corporation wartime Daimler CWA6 with a rebuilt Duple body working on the 75 route. It was fairly unusual for one of these buses to be found working on the jointly operated services. 2166 is passing Rhodes china ware shop, James Lister's engineering tools and lubricants premises and Proffitt & Westwood's pet supplies shop. (D.R. Harvey)

At 5.10 p.m. the conductor of the bus working on the 74 route waits for this turn's departure time to come around. 3170 (MOF 170), a Crossley-bodied Daimler CVG6, stands outside the Tower Café in Carter's Green on 27 March 1965. It was surprising in just how many places there was a café near to a Bundy Clock in the Birmingham City Transport operating area. This Hockley Garage-based bus is working back to West Bromwich and Birmingham. (J. Cockshot)

On 31 March 1939 Brush-built Car 597, destined to be the last tram to be broken up at Kyotts Lake Road Works on Thursday 6 August 1953, rattles across the points in Carter's Green as it works towards the stop alongside the Farley Clock. The tram is working on the Dudley-bound 74 route and will take the track going to the right alongside the parked West Bromwich-registered Ford 7W Tudor. (H.B. Priestley)

A line-up of five West Bromwich Corporation pre-war buses stand in Carter's Green waiting to resume their journeys back towards Dartmouth Square. All the buses are Daimler COG6s with Metro-Cammell H30/26R bodywork and are still painted in the livery which included the fleet name between the decks. There are a number of Union Jack flags being displayed suggesting that this is June 1953 and the flags are part of the celebrations for the Coronation of HM the Queen. (D. Williams)

A Travel West Midlands Alexander-bodied Dennis 'Trident', 4554 (BL 53 EER), travels away from the Farley Clock and the Black Country New Road in Carter's Green. On 25 January 2005 the bus is working on the 79 route from Wolverhampton and represents the type of buses used on this service since late 2003. Although the A41 West Bromwich bypass cut a swathe through the Guns Village area behind the bus, most of Carter's Green's original Victorian premises have survived, though Tower Cinema has long since been demolished. (D.R. Harvey)

The short working 73 tram route to Carter's Green terminated alongside the famous Farley Clock which had been erected in 1897 to recognise the philanthropic achievements of Reuben Farley (1826–1899) who had been Mayor of West Bromwich on five occasions. The brick-built clock tower is square and has four impressive clock faces. In 1937 Car 144 stands next to one of the newly erected Belisha Beacons, introduced in 1934 by the Transport Minister, the Right Hon. Leslie Hore-Belisha (1893–1957). The tram was re-motored in 1934 with a DK13A 40hp motor, and when it was withdrawn in September 1939 it became one of twenty-two of the 71 class retained in reserve throughout the Second World War. (R. Wilson)

Loading up outside Tower Cinema, Carter's Green is West Bromwich Corporation's 165 (GEA 165), a Weymann-bodied Daimler CVG6s of 1952, with an exposed radiator. This bus stop and concrete shelter were only used by the 75 service to Wednesbury and the 90 route operated by the West Bromwich and Wolverhampton Corporation. If the tramway takeover proposals of 1924 had reached a different conclusion regarding the operation of Birmingham Corporation trams as far as Bilston, rather than just to Wednesbury, then it might have been that the 75 bus service would have been jointly worked by Birmingham City Transport, West Bromwich and Wolverhampton Corporations. Tower Cinema was opened on 9 December 1935, and it is appropriate that the first film to be shown was Alfred Hitchcock's *The 39 Steps*, which starred Robert Donat and West Bromwich-born Madeleine Carroll. (D.R. Harvey)

Standing at the junction of Dudley Street and Old Meeting Street was the old Methodist Chapel which was opened in May 1876 and closed in 1949. The South Staffordshire Co. had opened the line to the White Horse at Wednesbury on 8 October 1903. In about 1914, about to turn from Old Meeting Street into Carter's Green, is a South Staffordshire Black Country Through Car. Car 31 was an open balcony still with open vestibules, leaving the driver (or motorman) open to the elements. This Brush-bodied tram mounted on Brush-built Lycett & Conaty Radial trucks, built in 1904, was formerly owned by either CBT or B&M and was transferred to SS especially to operate this service which opened on 8 October 1912. By 1914 the trams ran every sixteen minutes and took sixty-four minutes from Birmingham to Darlaston. To travel from Colmore Row to the Handsworth boundary cost 2d and, after re-booking at the Hawthorns, cost another 4½d to Darlaston. (Commercial Postcard)

A large totally enclosed Birmingham Corporation bogie car stands at the same spot in the shadow of the Farley Clock and the Methodist Chapel at Carter's Green, with Dudley Street going straight on to the left and Old Meeting Street to the right. In about 1930, tram 614, a Brush-built bogie car dating from the end of 1920, is travelling towards West Bromwich on the 75 service. Beneath the clock is the substantial passenger shelter which had been joined fairly recently by a K3 concrete telephone box. This had been designed by Sir Giles Gilbert Scott in 1929 with about 12,000 appearing over the country. (Commercial Postcard)

5

ON TO
WEDNESBURY

Having taken the turn from Carter's Green at the junction dominated by the Farley Clock, BCT Car 600 has taken the right-hand fork into Old Meeting Street as it heads towards Black Lake and Hill Top on the 75 service to Wednesbury. The tram was a Brush-bodied sixty-two-seater mounted on Brush-Burnley bogies. The tram entered service in the spring of 1920 with open balconies. Towards the end of the decade this class of tram was totally enclosed and upgraded by being fitted with a 63hp motor which made it ideal for the fast sections of track over the Sandwell Valley, Hill Top and beyond Carter's Green. The West Bromwich Corporation bus is 26 (EA 4194), a little Guy ONDF with a Guy B20F body dating from 1928. (D.R. Harvey Collection)

Passing the Classically styled Ebenezer Congregational Chapel dating from 1839 is West Bromwich Corporation 161 (GEA 161). This Daimler CVG6 had a Weymann H30/26R and entered service in 1952. It is travelling along Old Meeting Street from Black Lake towards Carter's Green, working on the 75 route in about 1961. Behind the bus on the corner of Church Lane is the 1920s-built King Edward VII public house. Travelling towards Wednesbury is a year-old Austin A55 van. (D. Wilson)

South Staffs Car 42 passes Hill Top Primary School with its pair of cupola bell-towers guarding the site, at the Coles Lane junction. These Victorian school buildings were demolished in 1994. The tram is travelling towards the steep descent of Holloway Bank as it goes on to Wednesbury. Almost certainly this is a Black Country Through Car which will terminate in Bilston. Car 42 was built as an open-top in 1904 by Brush for Birmingham & Midland Co. Known as the 'Aston' type, this tram was one of a number transferred to the South Staffs operation in 1912 in time for the introduction of the new service which originally terminated at Darlaston. (D.R. Harvey Collection)

Descending Holloway Bank towards the Wednesbury terminus is BCT eight-wheeled bogie Car 565. This tram is working on the 75 route on 31 March 1939 and has the abandonment notice in the balcony window. The steep 'S' bend from the Tame Valley had originally been developed for horse-drawn wagons to ease the climb up to Hill Top. This occurred during the mid-eighteenth century when Wednesbury was one of the world's largest producers of iron and subsequently steel tubes. By the 1930s the Depression had badly hit the town, and, with unemployment reaching over 30 per cent, the area was becoming very run-down. (R. T. Wilson)

The West Bromwich bus fleet was always immaculately maintained and the Corporation's livery of two shades of blue with yellow around the saloon windows and on the roof was a breath of fresh air in the frequently soot-covered Black Country. Climbing up the steep Holloway Bank, travelling towards Carter's Green on the 75 service in about 1954, is bus 78 (AEA 8). This was a Daimler COG6 with a Metro-Cammell H30/26R body which entered service in 1939 as one of the buses used to replace the trams. (A. Ingram)

Twenty-five years after 78 (AEA 8) climbed Holloway Bank, 3798 (NOV 798G) was doing the same. This was one of 100 Daimler 'Fleetline' CRG6LXs fitted with dual-door Park Royal H43/29D bodies. This bus entered service in December 1968 and was transferred to WMPTE on 1 October 1969. Here 3798 is wearing Birmingham's municipal crests, and is on Holloway Bank working on the 75 route between those dates. (D.R. Harvey Collection)

The White Horse in Bridge Street used to be one of the places where the magistrates met until 1846 when the Staffordshire Quarter Sessions built a courtroom in Russell Street. Standing outside the White Horse Hotel is 2190 (JOJ 190). The bus is a Leyland 'Titan' PD2/1 with a Park Royal H29/25R and was just seven months old when it was working on the 75 route on 13 June 1950. These powerful buses were fitted with the Leyland o.600 engine of 9.8 litres and with their synchromesh gearboxes were substantially quicker than other buses employed on the 74 or 75 routes. (G.F. Douglas, courtesy of A.D. Packer)

Hockley Garage did operate a batch of Crossley-bodied Daimler CVG6s which for many years were 3161–3179. 'New look'-fronted 3143 (MOF 143) entered service on 1 October 1953, and therefore was one of the class without the Coronation flag holders below the destination box. This bus was a late arrival at Hockley Garage having been one of Miller Street's vehicles for a long time. It is parked next to the Bundy Clock which was 'pegged' by the bus driver using his own unique key. This recorded a mark on a paper tape which could be checked to see if that duty left the terminus early, late or on time. Every Birmingham Corporation terminus had its own clock and was a feature of street furniture on routes operated by the Corporation. (A.D. Broughall)

Standing in front of the Georgian Lloyds Bank building at the junction of Holyhead Road and Lower High Street, Wednesbury, is one of the original South Staffordshire electric tramcars from the 40–55 class of open-top forty-seaters. These pioneering little double-deck tramcars opened both this, the Wednesbury to Bloxwich route, as well as the Darlaston to Mellish Road service, on 1 January 1893. The historical significance of this was that it was only the second system in Britain to use the overhead trolley method of current collection, and these sixteen trams operated some 7½ miles on these two routes. Towering over the tram is the tower and spire of St John's Church, which was built in 1846 and demolished in July 1985. (Commercial Postcard)

On the left is an unidentified South Staffordshire car at the terminus of the company service to Darlaston. BCT Car 613 stands at the awkwardly placed terminus of the 75 route from Colmore Row in Birmingham. The tram tracks in the foreground swinging to the left into Holyhead Road were originally used for the SS Black Country Through Car Service. This most useful route linked Birmingham to Bilston and was opened on 9 October 1912. Although offered to Birmingham to

operate, after reaching Darlaston with a bogie car, the link was severed here opposite the White Horse public house on 1 April 1924. The explanation given at the time was that the side-running overhead beyond Wednesbury was not suitable for Birmingham's trams, though the state of the worn tram tracks was probably the real reason. On the right is one of Walsall Corporation's 40–49 class. Built in 1919, this vestibule, open-balconied Brush-bodied 40hp four-wheeler only ran for fourteen years before the system closed on 30 September 1933. (Commercial Postcard)

Car 608 waits at the White Horse terminus of the 75 service in Wednesbury in 1935. The Wednesbury terminus for the Birmingham trams was also known as the White Horse, and they stopped almost outside this old Georgian hostelry. Tram 608 was a Brush totally enclosed eight-wheel tram, and entered service in 1920 with open upper saloon balconies, but in the late 1920s it had received a much more powerful 63hp motor, enclosed balcony and transverse lower saloon upholstered seating. Behind the tram

is Lower High Street, leading the short way to Wednesbury's attractive Victorian Market Place. Just visible is a Walsall Corporation Park Royal-bodied Dennis 'Lance'. (Commercial Postcard)

Turning right into Holyhead Road at the bottom of Lower High Street in Wednesbury is an early post-war Walsall Corporation bus. 100 (MDH 316), a Guy 'Arab' III 5LW with a very basically trimmed Park Royal H30/26R body from 1949, is working on the 37 route from Bradford Place, Walsall. On the right is Lloyds Bank's replacement 1950s building, and behind it is St John's Church. On the right, outside the White Horse public house, is West Bromwich Corporation's 172 (GEA 172). This unfortunate bus, a

Daimler CVG6 with a Weymann body, which entered service in March 1952, was bought for preservation but unfortunately was burnt out in 1975. (D. Wilson)

6

WHAT MIGHT HAVE BEEN THE ROUTE TO WOLVERHAMPTON

On the section of route over which Birmingham declined to operate trams after 1924, the first town of note to have been reached would have been Bilston. Standing at the junction with Frazer Street in Bilston is a post-war Wolverhampton Corporation trolleybus. Guy BT 492 (FJW 492), a 1949-built vehicle with a Park Royal H28/26R body, stands alongside posters advertising Marty Wilde's appearance at the Gaumont Cinema in 1958. 492 is working on the 7 route next to the tree-lined Methodist Chapel. (J.C. Brown)

At Bilston Town Hall outside Lloyds Bank, travelling towards Darlaston in 1927, is South Staffordshire Tramways Tramcar 37. This car was built by Brush in 1904 as one of the 'Aston' type, and is in the final rebuilt condition with temporary vestibule screens. The tram is working on the Wednesbury service after receiving an up-to-date GE 40hp motor. (D.R. Harvey)

South Staffordshire tramcar 41 stands at the terminus of the Wednesbury route in front of Bilston Town Hall when facing Darlaston and Wednesbury. On the right is a Tividale-built single-decker of the Wolverhampton District Company which is en route to the Fighting Cocks terminus in Wolverhampton. Car 41 was one of four of these Brush-built 'Aston'-type double-deckers which regularly performed on the Wednesbury, Darlaston-Bilston route. Seen in early 1928, this service was purchased by Wolverhampton Corporation on 1 September 1928, some six days after Wolverhampton had closed their own municipal system. It was a short-lived reprieve as the tram service was closed on 30 November 1928. (D.R. Harvey Collection, possibly A. Batty)

Waiting at the traffic lights at Mount Pleasant in Bilston is Alexander-bodied Dennis 'Trident' 4596 (BX 54 DCV). This bus is travelling towards Wolverhampton on the 79 route on 1 February 2005. The whole area was developed not long after the end of the Napoleonic Wars, during the Regency period, hence Wellington Road. Most of the buildings including the church are now Grade II listed. (D.R. Harvey)

Travelling from Bilston along Wellington Road at the junction with Wolverhampton Street Road is one of Wolverhampton's post-war trolleybuses. 614 (FJW 614), a 1949 vintage Sunbeam F4 with a Park Royal H28/26R, is working on the 2 service from Darlaston to Whitmore Reans. This cross-town route was opened on 27 January 1930 and continued unaltered until it was closed on 8 August 1965 and motorbuses took over. (C. Carter)

Under the trolleybus wires in Wellington Road at Wolverhampton traffic island is West Bromwich Corporation's 193 (PEA 193), one of a dozen Willowbrook-bodied Daimler CVG6s delivered in 1957. The bus is going towards Bilston on the 90 service in about 1958. This was a jointly operated service by West Bromwich and Wolverhampton Corporations. (A.B. Cross)

Wolverhampton Corporation's Bilston Road tram service terminated at the Bilston boundary at Stow Heath Lane. It was opened on 24 November 1902. Car 20, an ER&TCW open-top forty-eight-seater fitted with Lorain Surface Contact equipment, hence the lack of a trolleypole, stands opposite the Angel public house on the corner of Ward Street. On the other side of Stow Heath Lane is Wolverhampton District Car 19. This is a large Brush-built seventy-seat open-top bogie car also dating from 1902 and is waiting to return to Bilston. The through route was eventually converted to dual Lorain/overhead trams in 1905. (D.R. Harvey Collection)

Travelling towards the Priestfield tram stop on 15 February 2005 is Midland Metro Tram 15. It has just turned off Bilston Road near the junction with Ettingshall Road. Thus trams were brought back to Bilston Road on 31 May 1999. These Ansaldo 56 articulated single-deckers operate on the 12.28-mile Metro system between Snow Hill in Birmingham and St George's in Wolverhampton, mainly using the track bed of the old Great Western Railway line. (D.R. Harvey)

Travelling along Cleveland Road, working on the 90 route to West Bromwich, is Wolverhampton
Corporation 16 (SUK 16). This bus was a Guy 'Arab' IV with an MCCW H33/27R body
and, unusually, a Meadows 6DC engine. Had the through tram route from Birmingham been
implemented in 1924 the tram route would have left Wolverhampton along this stretch of road on
the way to Bilston. (D.R. Harvey Collection)

Speeding along Lichfield Street in the middle of Wolverhampton city centre is Travel West Midland's
4554 (BL 53 EER). Behind the bus is the Britannia Hotel and just visible to the immediate left of the
bus the splendidly restored Grand Theatre. This Dennis 'Trident', fitted with an Alexander H47/28F
body, dated from February 2004 and is working on the 79 route from Birmingham. The bus is about
to enter Wolverhampton's bus station on a route which was the successor to sections of historic tram,
trolleybus and bus routes linking Wolverhampton to Bilston, Darlaston, Wednesbury, West Bromwich and
Birmingham, but without ever having a single jointly operated through service. (D.R. Harvey)

7

CARTER'S GREEN
TO DUDLEY

Travelling along Dudley Street in about 1954 is BCT 2663 (JOJ 663). This Metro-Cammell-bodied Daimler CVD6 bus entered service in 1951 and is still wearing its original aluminium hub caps which were removed from all the 'new look'-fronted buses by about 1955 in order to ease maintenance costs. The bus has just left Carter's Green and is passing the Nags Head public house as it heads off towards Great Bridge on the 74 route. (D. Williams)

The first of the batch of thirty-one Daimler COG6s with Metro-Cammell H30/26R bodies was 72 (AEA 72). This bus was delivered in March 1939 in readiness for the tramway conversion and still retains the original livery layout which unusually had the gold fleet name located on the panels between the decks. It is in Dudley Street near to Carter's Green and is working on the 74 service in about 1954. Although the trams had been withdrawn fifteen years earlier, the bus is still riding next to the patched-up road surface and cobbled sets which marked the old tram tracks. (D. Williams)

Looking about as tired as its surroundings, 1768 (HOV 768), a 1948-vintage Daimler CVD6 with a Metro-Cammell H30/24R body, stands in the centre of Great Bridge on 24 March 1963, only five months before its withdrawal. The mid-nineteenth-century buildings in Great Bridge were rather down-at-heel although as a shopping centre it was still thriving. The bus is outside one of the butcher's shops owned by the Birmingham-based chain of J.H. Dewhurst with the grocer's shop owned by George Briscoe next door on the corner of Fisher Street. These premises had at one time been owned by the provision merchants Home and Colonial, who as well as selling sugar, coffee, butter and margarine, were best known for their selection of teas. (D. Wilson)

'Clara the Clairvoyant' seems to be doing a roaring trade among the canvas-covered stalls in Great Bridge Market Place, at a time when one's future might have been less than certain. Passing through in about 1941 is BCT's 250 (EOG 250). This Leyland 'Titan' TD6c had a Metro-Cammell H28/24R body. There were two seats less in the upper saloon to the contemporary Daimler COG5s because the weight of the torque converter gearbox pushed the unladen weight above the accepted level. The M&B public house dominating the centre of the Market Place is the Limerick, which was built originally as a hotel. Just behind its magnificent lantern is a West Bromwich Corporation Daimler COG6 double-decker. (D.R. Harvey Collection)

Turning round the back of the Limerick Hotel in the centre of Great Bridge is West Bromwich 143 (DEA 543). This Daimler CVG6 had a Metro-Cammell H30/26R body and entered service late in 1948. The 76 route was the Great Bridge short working of the main service to Dudley. On the right is Joseph Wiltshire's impressive outfitters shop. The road into which the bus is turning was at one time a narrow thoroughfare called Limerick Passage. In the inter-war years this was widened enabling the Market Place to be circumnavigated on both sides by traffic, replacing the two-way road behind this bus. (D. Wilson)

Passing through the railway bridge at Dudley Port was a tight fit for the Corporation trams. On 1 April 1939, just a few days before the abandonment of the 74 tram route, Dudley-bound bogie Car 619 begins its squeeze beneath the 16ft 4½in-high bridge. Trams were restricted to 4mph when passing through this bridge. The trams had to negotiate the single trackwork underneath the Ryland Aqueduct and the bridge carrying the LMS Railway through Dudley Port Station. The bridge was the lowest on the Birmingham tram system and the overhead wiring was placed wide of the track on the left side of the tram, thus pushing the tram's trolleypole below the level of the car's roof. (D. Clayton)

Travelling towards Horseley Heath on 74A route is WMPTE's 4143 (YOX 143K). This Daimler 'Fleetline' CRG6LX had an MCW H43/33F body and entered service in October 1971. In the distance is the Dudley Port Railway Bridge Station which opened on 1 July 1852 as one of the stations on the Stour Valley line of the Shrewsbury & Birmingham Railway (later LNWR) between Birmingham and Wolverhampton. Originally called High Level Station, it was unusually located on the railway bridge above the main road between Great Bridge and Dudley. The Low Level Station was opened in 1850 by the South Staffordshire Railway and closed by the Beeching Act in 1964. Behind the railway bridge is the Ryland Aqueduct which carried the Birmingham Canal. (D. Wilson)

On Thursday 14 April 1938 a heavily laden tramcar working on the 74 route from Birmingham passes the Atkinson Brewery-owned Waggon & Horses public house as it is climbs up Dudley Port towards Burnt Tree. Car 617, a Brush-bodied totally enclosed eight-wheel bogie car, dates from the end of 1920. The tram was re-motored in about 1928 with a 63hp DK30/1L motor which transformed her performance on the Dudley and Wednesbury services. Car 617 would finally run on 3 June 1953, the penultimate day of tramway operation in Birmingham. (H.B. Priestley)

Forty-eight years later, in July 1986, 6798 (SDA 798S) passes what used to be called the Waggon
& Horses. Today known as The Melting Pot, owned by Mitchells & Butlers Brewery, in this
photograph the pub still has its magnificent lantern over the front door. This bus, a Leyland
'Fleetline' FE30AGR with an MCW H43/33F body dating from May 1978, is travelling towards
Dudley working on the 74 service. (D.R. Harvey)

The distant Dudley Port public house was just on the Horseley Heath side of Sedgley Road.
WMPTE's 4103 (YOX 103K), one of West Bromwich Garage's Daimler 'Fleetline' CRG6LXs
with a Park Royal body dated from 1971, works away from Dudley on the 74 route in about
1978. (B.J. Whitelaw)

THE CAPE HILL, SMETHWICK, OLDBURY AND DUDLEY ROUTE

The history of the tram services between Birmingham, Smethwick, Oldbury and Dudley began when Birmingham & Midland Tramway Co. was instigated on 22 November 1883. The lease on the lines within the Birmingham boundary was to be held until June 1906 while those beyond Grove Lane were to be operated on lines built by Birmingham & Western District Tramways Co. The B&MT opened their steam-powered tramway on 6 July 1885 from Lionel Street to the Grove Lane town boundary. By August 1885 the trams were operating through Smethwick to Oldbury, and on 30 August 1885 a one-hour service to Dudley Station was established. Although the steam trams were successful, in August 1899 BET gained control of the B&MT with the intention of electrifying the route.

The 8-mile line to Dudley was opened for electric trams on 21 November 1904 and was operated by the company from their converted steam tram depot at West Smethwick. The branch to Bearwood from Cape Hill was also opened on this date while the Heath Street branch inside the Birmingham boundary was opened on 31 December 1904 and extended over the boundary in Cranford Street on company-owned tracks to Soho Station on 24 May 1905. When the lease on the lines within the city expired on 30 June 1906, Corporation tramcars took over the operation of the routes to Bearwood and Soho, which in 1915 were given the route numbers 29 and 31 respectively, while the short working to Windmill Lane was numbered 30. The Dudley Road route to the city boundary at Grove Lane was given the route number 55. The new tram depot in Rosebery Street was opened on 14 April 1906 for the Lodge Road trams, and it was from here that the new Birmingham Corporation trams were operated.

The company continued to operate from Dudley and Oldbury to the new terminus in Margaret Street on 1 July 1906, along with the routes now solely operated by BCT. Meanwhile, the B&MT had opened its new depot and works at Tividale, just before Burnt Tree, on 1 January 1907. The company cars, after August 1912 owned by the renamed Birmingham District Power & Traction Co., continued running from the mainline tram service through Smethwick and Oldbury to Dudley on the route which was given the nickname of 'The Track'.

On 1 April 1928, after negotiations were quite quickly instigated by Birmingham District, Birmingham Corporation took over the running of all the tram routes previously operated by the company, including those beyond Cape Hill. The Birmingham District's reasoning was that they would have had to invest quite quickly in a fleet of new tramcars to replace their original 1904 fleet, and, after initially being quite enthusiastic in the autumn of 1927, completely rethought their policy. Another factor was that the lease for the tramlines was to expire on 31 December 1938, and the expensive capital outlay for new trams would not be worth it for just ten years. Having agreed to take over the operation, the Corporation was so short of trams that they had to hire some thirty-eight Birmingham District trams, some of which were not returned until 15 October 1928. By this date the fifty new 762-811 class of bogie cars had been delivered to Washwood Heath Depot, and this enabled the 71 class of ex-Radial-trucked four-wheelers to be transferred to both Rosebery Street and the taken-over West Smethwick Depot.

For the next ten years 'The Track' was successfully operated by BCT, but the local authorities of Smethwick, Oldbury, Rowley Regis, Tipton and Dudley compulsorily purchased the tramways under the terms of the 1870 Tramways Act at the end of 1938. BCT entered into an agreement to

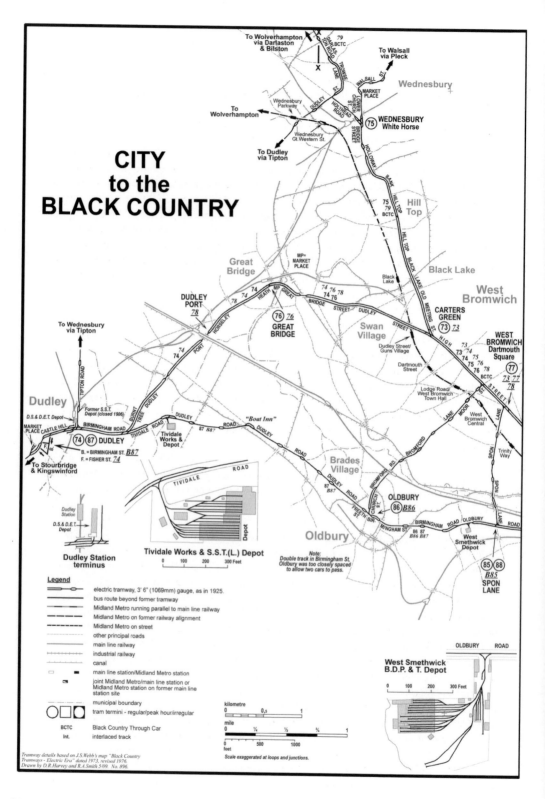

CITY
to the
BLACK COUNTRY

Legend

	electric tramway, 3' 6" (1069mm) gauge, as in 1925.
	bus route beyond former tramway
	Midland Metro running parallel to main line railway
	Midland Metro on former railway alignment
	Midland Metro on street
	other principal roads
	main line railway
	industrial railway
	canal
	main line station/Midland Metro station
	joint Midland Metro/main line station or Midland Metro station on former main line station site
	municipal boundary
	tram termini - regular/peak hour/irregular
BCTC	Black Country Through Car
Int.	interlaced track

Dudley Station terminus

Dudley Station
D.S.& D.E.T. Depot

Tividale Works & S.S.T.(L.) Depot
TIVIDALE ROAD
Depot
0 100 200 300 Feet

West Smethwick B.D.P. & T. Depot
OLDBURY ROAD
0 100 200 300 Feet

Note:
Double track in Birmingham St, Oldbury was too closely spaced to allow two cars to pass.

kilometre
0   0,5   1

mile
0   ¼   ½   ¾   1

feet
0   500   1000

Scale exaggerated at loops and junctions.

Tramway details based on J.S.Webb's map "Black Country Tramways - Electric Era" dated 1973, revised 1976. Drawn by D.R.Harvey and R.A.Smith 5/09. No. 896.

continue operating the trams for another twelve months, but the condition of the track was so poor beyond the city boundary that it speeded up the decision to abandon the trams, which was keenly desired by the Black Country local authorities through which the trams operated. The closure of the Black Country tram services was set for 30 September 1939, and although the Second World War was three weeks underway, the abandonment was completed. BCT had briefly flirted with keeping the Dudley Road section to the Grove Lane boundary open, but as replacement buses were delivered this idea was quietly dropped. The replacement bus services were all given the pre-fix B, so the B80 went to Grove Lane, B81 to Windmill Lane, B82 to Bearwood, the B83 to Soho, B84 to St Paul's Road, B85 to Spon Lane, B86 to Oldbury and finally the B87 to Dudley.

The Corporation ran the services to Soho and Bearwood while they also did a few turns to Windmill Lane, St Paul's Road and Spon Lane, but the B86 and B87 routes were the total preserve of Midland Red. BMMO operated their brand new fleet of fifty SOS FEDDs, numbered between 2332 and 2381, from Oldbury Garage, which had opened on 12 April 1937. The Birmingham Corporation replacement buses were fifty vehicles, this time Leyland-bodied Leyland 'Titan' TD6cs, operated until 1947 by Hockley Garage, after which the abandonment of the Ladywood 33 route on 30 August 1947 meant these buses could be operated from Rosebery Street Garage.

Between December 1949 and March 1950 some twenty-six of the handsome but totally non-standard Park Royal-bodied Leyland 'Titan' PD2/1s arrived at Rosebery Street Garage, encouraging the idea that the Dudley Road bus services were a separate enclave within the Corporation's operations. Between January and March 1952 another twenty new buses arrived, these being the last of the Daimler-engined Daimler CVD6 with 'new look' concealed radiators and Metro-Cammell triple destination boxes. As if to continue the illusion of the separateness of the Dudley Road routes, these CVD6s always ran with the front number boxes blanked out.

Meanwhile the Midland Red buses were gradually being renewed. The pre-war FEDD buses were slowly replaced until, in 1959, they were the largest surviving allocation on the BMMO system. The last FEDDs were withdrawn in December 1960 and replaced mainly with BMMO D7s, although some D5s and D5Bs had been at the garage since the mid-1950s. The final D7 was taken out of service by early 1972.

By the time WMPTE took over the Midland Red operations on 3 December 1973, Oldbury was running some twenty-two BMMO D9s, which for many years were not operated as an agreement with BCT precluded their use because of their high seating capacity. A variety of Alexander-bodied Daimler 'Fleetlines' also went to Oldbury, many of which continued working at the garage after the takeover.

A number of former Birmingham MOF-registered Guy 'Arab' IVs worked in 1971, while later some Daimler CVG6s with Crossley bodies and Coventry Daimler CVG6s were transferred to Oldbury to work mainly on the 82 route. Some of the former Walsall Corporation forward entrance Willowbrook-bodied Dennis 'Loline' IIs came and went in the mid-1970s, but from 1971 standard WMPTE YOX-registered Daimler 'Fleetlines' arrived. The D9 allocation stayed at about this number until January 1976 when the Ailsa buses began to replace them. Perhaps some of the most distinctive modern buses to be operated on the B87 service were thirty of the 1976 batch of WMPTE-owned Ailsa B55-10s with Alexander H44/35F bodies. Oldbury Garage closed in 1986 and their duties were split between Quinton and West Bromwich garages until the former was shut in March 1997 and all the Oldbury services moved to Oak Lane.

After deregulation in 1986 many operators have appeared on the Dudley Road services. The most successful has been Black Diamond Buses, formerly Birmingham Coach Co., though Pete's Travel and the Thandi Group have also operated on the shorter services to Smethwick. Since July 2006 a new fleet of eighteen buses have been purchased by Travel West Midlands for use on both the 82 route to Bearwood and the 87 route to Dudley. These were Volvo B7TLs with Wright Gemini H43/29F bodies, and in the twenty-first century were an amazing advance on the original steam trams which began public transport 121 years before these Volvo buses were put on the road.

1 **2** **3**

DUDLEY ROAD

1 BMMO 2d Adult shortworking
   post-9/1939
2 BMMO 2½d Adult City outer
3 BMMO 4d Adult shortworking
   post-9/1939
4 BCT 1½d Child crossing City boundary
5 BCT 4d Adult crossing City boundary
6 BCT & O 2½d Adult outside City
   boundary 1928-1937
7 BCT 1½d Adult outside City boundary
   post-1937

4 **5**

6 **7**

SOHO ROAD

8 BCT 1d Adult cross boundary
9 BCT 1d Child cross boundary
10 BCT 1½d Adult cross boundary
11 BCT 2d Adult cross boundary
12 West Bromwich 1½d Adult cross
   boundary
13 BCT 2½d Adult cross boundary
14 BCT 8d Workman's cross boundary
15 BCT & O Chambon 1934
16 BCT Tramways 1d Child Standard
   post-1924
17 BCT & O 2d Adult 1927-1937

8 **9** **10** **11**

12 **13** **14**

15 **16** **17**

8

BIRMINGHAM CITY CENTRE

Waiting in Smallbrook Queensway at the entrance to New Street Station on 23 July 2007 is 4706 (BU 06 CWZ). This is a Volvo B7TL with a Wright H43/29F body which entered service in August 2006. Because of the curved shape of the windscreen, the Wright-bodied buses were quickly nicknamed 'Nokia Buses' due to their similarity to the shape of that manufacturer's mobile telephones. Like most of these eighteen double-deckers, 4706 is route-branded for the Dudley Road services and is working on the 87 service via Oldbury to Dudley. To the left is the new Bull Ring Shopping Centre, opened on 4 September 2003 at a cost of £800 million. (D.R. Harvey)

Picking up passengers on Great Charles Street is 6268 (YHA 268J). This was when the inbound Dudley Road route travelled down to Snow Hill Circus in order to get into the centre of Birmingham. This former Midland Red-owned Daimler 'Fleetline' CRG6LX entered service in December 1970, new to Oldbury Garage. On 14 June 1978 this attractive Alexander-bodied two-door seventy-five-seater, by now repainted in WMPTE colours, is working on the 85 route from Spon Lane. It remained in service until January 1981. (A.B. Cross)

Margaret Street was cut in 1883 between Edmund Street and Cornwall Street, replacing numerous dilapidated Georgian houses clustered around unsanitary courtyards and alleyways. The lovely art nouveau-style Birmingham College of Arts and Crafts was completed in 1885 to the design of J.H. Chamberlain, who died at the age of fifty-two before even the foundation stone had been laid. Margaret Street was used by the Dudley Road group of tram services from 1906 as part of a terminal loop giving them access to the impressive passenger shelters in Edmund Street. After the closure of the Dudley Road tram services in September 1939, the loop was still used by the replacing buses. Having unloaded outside the college, a Midland Red BMMO D7 bus, 4533 (XHA 533), is working on the 86 service to Oldbury. (D.R. Harvey Collection)

On 1 April 1928 BCT took over the operation of the Smethwick, Oldbury and Dudley sections of the route outside the city boundary as well as acquiring West Smethwick Depot. This extra work resulted in an acute shortage of tramcars. As some of the track beyond Cape Hill was poor, the only suitable Corporation trams were the already quite elderly 71-class cars. These were mainly going to come from Washwood Heath Depot where they were due to be replaced by new 762-class bogie cars. As a result of this shortage, the first 71-class trams could not be transferred to the Dudley Road services (operated by Rosebery Street Depot) until August 1928. The

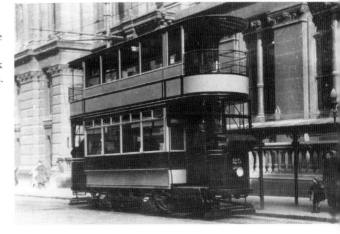

Corporation therefore had little alternative but to hire thirty-eight of the most serviceable Birmingham & District tramcars at a rate of £3 per week per car from the date of the changeover until 15 October 1928 when the last of the Birmingham District cars went to Darlaston for scrapping by the company. In about 1927, Tividale-built Car 29, originally an open-top but now a respectable 35hp top-covered tram, stands at the Edmund Street terminus of the Dudley route. (A.D. Packer Collection)

The Second World War was just over three weeks old on Saturday 30 September 1939 when a line of four trams stood at the impressive loading shelters on Edmund Street at the terminus of the Dudley Road tram services. On the left, outside the Gas Hall in the Council House Extension, the building is protected by serried ranks of sandbags. Other wartime precautions were already installed, with the street furniture, kerbs and edges of the trams and the cars already painted white while on the right a signpost points to the nearest ARP air-raid shelter. This was the last day of tramcar operation on these routes. The leading tram is working on the 85 service to Spon Lane. It is an open-balconied ex-Radial truck, Car 209, built by UEC in 1907, which would be withdrawn at the end of this day and placed in store at Rosebery Street Depot as a reserve car for the rest of the war. (D.R. Harvey Collection)

The Dudley Road bus services operated by Birmingham City Transport came under the fiefdom of Rosebery Street Garage, for their operation was akin to a kingdom within an empire. This was in the main due to the vehicles it operated, and for twenty-nine years the bulk of these were either pre-war Leyland 'Titan' TD6cs with Leyland bodies or the equally none-BCT-looking Park Royal Leyland 'Titan' PD2/1s of 1950. 2217 (JOJ 217) was one of the latter, and these attractively-bodied buses were the stalwarts of Rosebery Street's operations. It is at the Edmund Street terminus of the B82 service, before 1953 as it is not fitted with a Coronation flag holder which would have been placed in the centre of the thin blue livery line above the windscreen in that year. (S.N.J. White)

Although not a common occurrence, Midland Red did operate a percentage of buses on the B82 route to Bearwood by way of Dudley Road and Cape Hill. Standing beneath the large Romanesque-styled bridge over Edmund Street, which was opened in 1912 and connects the Art Gallery to the Council House Extension, is BMMO D7 4371 (VHA 371). In about 1959 this Metro-Cammell-bodied bus waits to load up under the watchful eye of its conductor who is standing on the still-cobbled road. The D7s, while not as comfortable as the Corporation's buses, did seat four more passengers, had platform doors and heaters. (L. Mason)

Rosebery Street had the last twenty of the 1952 batch of Metro-Cammell-bodied Daimler CVD6s, operating them until the garage closed in June 1968. The last of the batch, 2775 (JOJ 775), entered service on 25 March 1952 and is seen here turning out of Edmund Street in November 1961, working on the B82 service to Bearwood by way of Dudley Road and Cape Hill. (D. Williams)

The Portland stonework on the Council House Extension was designed in the Edwardian Renaissance by architects Ashley and Newman, and was begun in 1912, but, because of the First World War, was not completed until 1919. It still looks new when compared to the distant Art Gallery clock tower, known as 'Big Brum', which was built in 1885 to the design of Yeoville Thomason, who was also responsible for the adjoining Council House in Victoria Square. Travelling along Congreve Street is Birmingham & Midland Car 36, though when the Corporation took over operation of the Smethwick, Oldbury and Dudley tram routes on 1 April 1928, this tram was not one of the thirty-eight company cars hired by the municipal operator. (Commercial Postcard)

The successor to the 32 tram service to Winson Green and Lodge Road was the 96 route. Unlike the little Brill-Maley four-wheeled open-balconied trams with a seating capacity of only forty-eight, which had disappeared in March 1947, only fifteen years later the route was operating the newest and largest capacity buses in the Corporation's bus fleet. The 96 service shared the Edmund Street terminus with the Dudley Road services and followed those routes to the Parade where it turned up Newhall Hill and into Birmingham's famous Jewellery Quarter. An inbound 3239 (239 DOC), a Leyland 'Atlantean' PDR1/1 with a seventy-two-seat Metro-Cammell body, approaches the traffic lights at the top of Summer Row before turning left as a Hillman Minx Phase V car crosses Great Charles Street. Behind the 'Atlantean' is a Park Royal-bodied Leyland 'Titan' PD2/1 working on the B82 Bearwood service. (D. Williams)

Coming over the crest of the hill at the top of Summer Row, just beyond Lionel Street and about to pass the 1930s-built Civic House, is 1277 (FOF 277), working on the B83 route from Bearwood. This bus is a Leyland 'Titan' TD6c with a Leyland H28/24R body which entered service on 1 September 1939 and was one of the first of the fifty-strong class to be withdrawn on 30 November 1950. Behind the bus are the premises of Brightside Foundry & Engineering Co. at 17 Summer Row. (D. Griffiths)

Nearly all of the turns on the B85 route to Spon Lane were undertaken by Midland Red, with the services being operated by Oldbury Garage. Climbing into Summer Row from the distant Parade and passing the Friday Bridge premises of Charles Edkins' metal button works is Midland Red's 3788 (NHA 788), a BMMO D5B with a Brush H30/26R body which had been built with the luxury of platform doors. (A.B. Cross)

A rather full-up 2766 (JOJ 766), a Daimler CVD6 with an MCCW H30/24R body, is starting out from the city centre and is about halfway down the steep Parade. It has crossed the Birmingham & Fazeley Canal's Saturday Bridge at Summer Row at the top of the hill. Saturday Bridge was so-called because it was where the bargees got paid every Saturday. The bus is working on the B82 service to Bearwood in about 1959. (L. Mason)

As it travels out of the city, Car 196 crosses the junction in the Parade with the tracks coming out of Newhall Hill from the Jewellery Quarter. On the right are the early Victorian premises at 66 Parade of Hoyle, Robson Barnett – paint manufacturers. On Wednesday 12 April 1939, Car 196 is working on the 80 route to St Paul's Road, Smethwick. In the distance is Car 53, one of the small UEC-built forty-eight-seaters fitted with Maley brakes and bow-collectors for the tortuous 32 service to Lodge Road. (H.B. Priestley)

Passing the premises of Richmond Rubber Co. between Newhall Hill and Camden Street in the Parade is BCT bus 1285 (FOF 285). This Leyland 'Titan' TD6c with a Leyland H28/26R body entered service on 1 September 1939 and would remain in use until 31 October 1952, but unlike most of the fifty-strong class this particular bus was sold to W.T. Bird in Stratford and immediately broken up. 1285 is working on the B82 route from Bearwood in 1949. (D. Griffiths)

Low-height Car 309 has cleared the Camden Street junction in the Parade working on the 29 route from Bearwood on 6 April 1939. The tram is passing the premises of George Baines' model bakery. Car 309 was a UEC-bodied 40hp tram fitted with a 7ft 6in wheelbase truck. It had only just been transferred from Selly Oak Depot, but its operational sojourn at Rosebery Street would be brief, although after the abandonment of the Dudley Road routes it would remain in store at that depot until May 1940. This tram had entered service in the spring of 1911 and would become one of the last group of four-wheel trams to remain in service as it survived until 30 September 1950, with the closure of the Washwood Heath tram services. (L.W. Perkins)

A Midland Red D5 with Brush H30/26R bodywork dating from 1949 travels into Birmingham working on the B87 route from Dudley and Oldbury. This Oldbury-garaged bus is passing the Nurses Home owned by the then Birmingham Public Health Department. This building was demolished in 2008. Hidden by the bus is the College Garage and petrol filling station and the premises of W.J. Ganes, funeral directors. (R.H.G. Simpson)

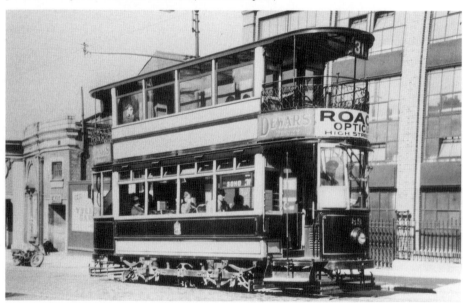

Car 89 picks up passengers in Summer Hill on 12 April 1939 as it travels into Birmingham. It is at the Bulpitts hollow-ware factory about 100 yards on the city side of the Icknield Street junction. The tram is working on the short 31 branch off Dudley Road to Soho by way of Heath Street. This fifty-two-seat tram was built by UEC in 1906 and was originally fitted with Mountain & Gibson 8ft 6in wheelbase Radial trucks. This tram was subsequently one of just nine of the class to be fitted with a Brush truck of similar wheelbase. (L.W. Perkins)

9

SUMMER HILL TO THE CAPE OF GOOD HOPE

One of the worst accidents in Birmingham involving a bus occurred on 16 March 1949. The bus, 1041 (CVP 141), a 1937 Daimler COG5, was travelling across Spring Hill into Icknield Street, working on the Inner Circle 8 route, when it was hit by a speeding fire engine and finished up on its side alongside the impressive Gothic-styled Spring Hill Library, which itself dates from January 1893. Ten passengers were killed as the offside of the bus' lower saloon was ripped out. Needless to say, the stricken 1041 was subsequently scrapped. (Birmingham Central Library)

On 5 August 1968, 2218 (JOJ 218), a Leyland 'Titan' PD2/1 with a Park Royal H29/25R body, stands in Spring Hill just beyond the Ladywood Middleway junction, with the large tower of Spring Hill Library on the opposite side of the road. By this time Rosebery Street Garage had been closed for about five weeks and the surviving PD2/1s were being operated by Quinton Garage where they were not much liked as they had synchromesh manual gearboxes rather than the preselector gearboxes fitted to Quinton's normal Guy 'Arab' III Specials and 'Arab' IVs. The transfer of the routes to Quinton also meant the loss of the B prefix to the Dudley Road services, hence 2217 displaying 82 as the route number. (G. Yates)

Rosebery Street Depot was opened on 14 April 1906 initially to operate the Lodge Road route. After 1 July of the same year the Bearwood and Soho routes were introduced while subsequently the Ladywood and Hagley Road routes were operated, giving the depot an allocation of about seventy-five trams. One of the three-bay UEC-bodied Brill-Maley trams, Car 50, used on the Lodge Road route and fitted with a bow-collector, has just returned to the depot on 17 June 1939, having travelled from Spring Hill by way of College Street. (L. W. Perkins)

The final day of tram operation at Rosebery Street Depot was 30 August 1947. On that day UEC open-balcony Car 345, the penultimate tram on the Ladywood route, and behind it Car 319, which actually closed the 33 route, stand withdrawn in the depot. They were still painted in wartime grey livery and were two of the last five 301 class not to be repainted in fleet livery. Both of these trams had come from Miller Street Depot on the previous day in order to specifically close the 33 route. The totally enclosed bogie car on the left, Car 736, would be moved to Selly Oak on the following day. The bus on the right is 'torque' Leyland 1312 (FOF 312), while parked over the pits at the rear of the premises is the identical 1292 (FOF 292), which like the bus in the foreground still wears its wartime livery. Rosebery Street closed as a bus garage on 29 June 1968 (C.C. Thornburn)

Turning from Spring Hill into College Street in late 1946 is Car 55, returning to the depot. This was one of seventeen Brill-Maley cars retained at Rosebery Street Depot for use on the Lodge Road 32 service. Because of the tight turns on the route, the trams with their short 6ft wheelbase trucks were fitted with Rowland Skate bow-collectors. The tall nave just beyond College Street was a Baptist Chapel, while on the extreme left is the Old College Inn. (J.S. Webb)

Passing the Walton Road fish and chip shop beyond Eyre Street at the top of Spring Hill is the unique BCT bus 1235 (FOF 235). The Daimler COG5 chassis was placed in service on 16 November 1939 with the penultimate Metro-Cammell H30/24R body to be built to Birmingham's pre-war specification. Towards the end of 1945, BCT commissioned a prototype post-war body from Brush, the Loughborough coachbuilder. 1235's old body was removed in late February 1946 and, after the chassis was refurbished, it went to Brush and the 'new' bus entered service on 1 May 1946. One feature of the body not perpetuated was the huge destination boxes whose apertures were quickly reduced to cater for the standard-size destination blinds. Between 1958 and 1960 the bus was allocated to Rosebery Street where it was a regular performer on the B82 route and, as here, the B80 short working to Grove Lane. (L. Mason)

Car 180 is being held up by the BCT Tilling-Stevens TS3 Tower Wagon 7 (O 9922). This vehicle had been originally purchased by Midland Red in March 1913 and was acquired by BCT on 5 October 1914. After withdrawal as a thirty-four-seat open-top double-decker in November 1924, it was converted to this state exactly a year later and lasted as a tower wagon until November 1934. On Thursday 6 October 1932 the tram is waiting on the Spring Hill canal bridge over the Soho Loop Canal, working on the 29 route to Bearwood. (D.R. Harvey Collection)

Travelling across the long Lee Bridge above the deep cutting over both the Birmingham Canal and the mainline railway line between Birmingham and Wolverhampton is Midland Red's 4099 (THA 99). This BMMO D7 had a Metro-Cammell H32/26R body and entered service in 1953. It is working on the B87 route to Dudley, a route which still retained the old tramway nickname of 'The Track'. Behind the bus are the old buildings which for many years were part of the Dudley Road Hospital complex. The hospital started life as the Birmingham Union Infirmary, being erected in 1889, as an extension to the workhouse in Western Road from designs by W.H. Ward, and it had a corridor a ¼ mile long, linking nine pavilions, based on a model recommended by Florence Nightingale. (M. Collignon)

Travelling into Birmingham on 24 October 1964 are two stalwarts of Rosebery Street Garage, both buses working on the B82 route from Bearwood. Beginning to cross Lee Bridge in Dudley Road is 2769 (JOJ 769), a 'new look'-fronted Daimler CVD6 with an MCCW H30/24R body. Following behind, having just crossed the Heath Street junction, is 2230 (JOJ 230), the last of fifty Park Royal-bodied Leyland PD2/1s dating from 1950. (W. Ryan)

The 31 route required only two trams to maintain the off-peak service on this 1¼-mile branch off Dudley Road along Heath Street to Soho Station. The tram coming out of Heath Street and crossing the Belisha crossing in the shadow of the M&B-owned Lee Bridge Tavern is ex-Radial Car 89. 30 September 1939 was the final day of the Dudley Road trams and, with the Phoney War just over three weeks old, the deep stack of sandbags in Heath Street are in evidence. (L.W. Perkins)

At the far end of the short route along Heath Street to Soho Station, 2214 (JOJ 214) stands on the bridge over the Stour Valley main line. The station closed in 1949 although the electrified railway line from New Street to Wolverhampton and beyond runs passed the now totally unidentifiable site of the station. The bus route now numbered B83 waits just in front of the concrete Midland Red bus shelter. The bus is one of Rosebery Street Garage's Leyland 'Titan' PD2/1s with a Park Royal H29/25R body. (L. Mason)

Working on the 55 route to the city boundary at Grove Lane is Brush totally enclosed Car 539. This tramcar had been transferred to Rosebery Street Depot from Hockley in 1935 and stayed until the closure of the Ladywood 33 route on 30 August 1947. On 9 April 1939 the tram is in Dudley Road, near to the junction with Icknield Port Road, which was the terminus of the Ladywood tram route. The three-storey shop premises on the left date from the 1870s and surprisingly are still there in 2009. (D. Clayton)

When almost new, in 1907, and in its original condition with open vestibules and a destination box immediately above the driver's head, Car 175 has just passed the Winson Green Road junction opposite Summerfield Park, which opened in 1876. There is some maintenance to a tramway traction pole taking place alongside the park's stone wall, judging by the size of the enormous ladder. The 71–220 class were built with Mountain & Gibson Radial trucks which, after a few years in service, experienced a lack of return action after taking a curve. 135 cars of the class were re-trucked with, including 175, Brush Peckham P35 units. (W. Hutt)

In about 1974, in early WMPTE days, 4949 (4949 HA), a Midland Red BMMO D9 double-decker with seventy-two seats, stands at the rudimentary bus shelter outside Summerfield Park. A Reliant three-wheel van is coming out of Winson Green Road on the left. The bus, about to be overtaken by a Riley Elf, a more luxurious version of the Mini but with an extended boot, is working on an 87 turn to Dudley. 4949 had been at Bearwood for its entire Midland Red career, which had begun in February 1962, and was one of twenty-two D9s taken over by WMPTE. 4949 survived with West Midlands until 1976, having been repainted into the blue and cream livery of its new owners. (D.R. Harvey)

The latest generation of vehicles being used on the Dudley Road services are eighteen Volvo B7TLs with Wright Eclipse H43/29F bodies, all of which entered service in 2006. 4717 (BU 06 CXM) passes through the Victorian-built shopping area in the quite narrow section of Dudley Road near the Grove Lane junction. The bus is working on the 87 route to Dudley on 2 March 2009. (D.R. Harvey)

From the bottom of Cape Hill at the city boundary to Dudley was 6.17 route-miles. The conductor of Car 124 has turned the trolleypole prior to the tram being driven over the crossover and on to the left-hand track before returning to Birmingham on the 55 route. This tram was an open-balcony Radial truck built by UEC in late 1906. It was one of 150 trams constructed at this time and although top-covered with a seating capacity of fifty-two, they were, at 16ft high, unable to pass beneath some bridges on the BCT system. This was a contributory factor to the withdrawal of all the 71-class trams by September 1939. To the right, on the corner of Grove Lane, is the Cape of Good Hope public house, designed by pub architects Wood & Kendrick and opening on 23 December 1925 to replace an old ale house on the same site. This building was closed on 7 July 1994 and replaced by a McDonalds. (W.A. Camwell)

Having climbed back into his cab after pegging the Bundy Clock at the Dudley Road boundary stop, the driver of 1272 (FOF 272) gets himself set before driving back to Edmund Street in Birmingham's city centre. The bus is working on the B82 service from Bearwood, and behind this Leyland-bodied Leyland 'Titan' TD6c is a Midland Red SOS FEDD working on the B86 route from Oldbury. Towering above the Corporation bus is the Grove Cinema which was opened on 22 August 1932 and closed on 24 October 1981 when it was converted into a furniture shop. (F.W. York)

Shortly before the world famous Mitchells & Butlers Brewery was demolished in early 2005, MCW 'Metrobus' Mk II, 2879 (B879 DOM), starts the climb up Cape Hill from the junction at Grove Lane. The bus is working on the 82 route to Bearwood. It is passing the impressive warehouses of the brewery. Henry Mitchell opened the original Crown Brewery on Cape Hill in July 1879 and the site was extensively enlarged until the 1970s when, for a time, M&B were the world's largest producers of real ale. Unfortunately successive take-overs, rationalisations and sheer bad management decisions led to the brewery finally closing on 6 December 2002. (R. Weaver)

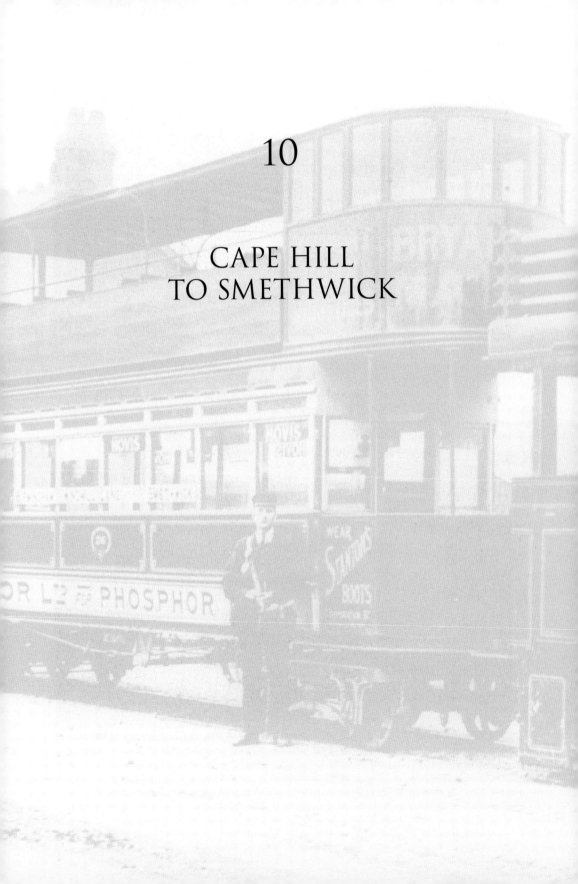

10

CAPE HILL
TO SMETHWICK

The steep descent down Cape Hill took the trams and later the buses from 557ft at the summit at Windmill Lane to 465ft at the Grove Lane junction. Birmingham & Midland Car 29 travels down Cape Hill passing the rows of Victorian shops which were such an important feature of this part of the route. Car 29 originally dates from 1904 as an open-top forty-eight-seater and was one of sixty-eight Brush-built 'Aston'-type trams constructed for B&M and CBT in Birmingham. Top-covered in 1908 and re-trucked and re-motored just after the First World War, Car 29 was one of the thirty-eight B&M trams hired by Birmingham Corporation after the takeover of the Oldbury and Dudley services on 1 April 1928. (D.R. Harvey Collection)

Climbing up Cape Hill on 2 March 2003 is 1556 (R556 XOB). This Mercedes-Benz-bodied single-decker 0405N seating forty-three passengers entered service in June 1998. It was one of 193 delivered in two batches to TWM between February 1998 and December 1999, comprising the largest order for this very common European bus placed in the UK. 1556 is working on the M80 route operating between Birmingham, Smethwick, West Bromwich, Hill Top and Wednesbury. The M prefix indicates that it serves the Midland Metro, in this case in West Bromwich. (D.R. Harvey)

The busy shopping centre at the top of Cape Hill was, looking towards Birmingham, dominated by the large Seven Stars Hotel with its ornate lantern over the main doorway on the corner of Windmill Lane, on the left. On the extreme right is Waterloo Road, which took the Corporation's 29 tram route to Bearwood. Most of the shops on this early 1920s summer day have their canvas blinds pulled down giving cool shade to the inside of the shop in these pre-refrigeration or air-conditioned days. In the distance, passing the tower of the Renaissance-style Barclays Bank on the corner of Salisbury Road, are two B&M tramcars from the 19–50 batch of Brush-built 'Aston'-type four-wheelers. (Commercial Postcard)

The imposing Lloyds Bank at the apex of Bearwood Hill and Waterloo Road was built in 1907 and replaced a large Georgian house called the Elms. In about 1930, BCT Car 72, standing at the Windmill Road junction, has arrived on an 80 route short working from St Paul's Road, Smethwick. Behind the tramcar is Bearwood Hill with a row of three-storey Victorian shops with gabled attics. (Commercial Postcard)

At the junction of Bearwood Hill and Waterloo Road until 1906 was a large eighteenth-century house, appropriately named The Elms. On the left is Waterloo Road which unlike the rest of the Cape Hill area was lined with houses rather than shops. The tram route to Windmill Lane was opened on 21 November 1904 while the tracks to Bearwood on the left opened just three days later. The leading tram showing 'WINDMILL LANE' on the destination box is B&M 22. This Brush-built 'Aston'-type open-top tramcar was delivered at the same time as the route opening in 1904. The second open-top tram negotiating the cross-over is CBT Car 214 which was on loan in the spring of 1905 to B&M, who were short of new tramcars. Car 214 would eventually become BCT's 483, having been completely rebuilt with a top-cover and vestibule platform, and it lasted until withdrawal in March 1939, thus almost surviving throughout the life of the electric tram services on Dudley Road. (D.R. Harvey Collection)

Loading up with passengers at Cape Hill in about 1906 is B&M open-top Car 13. These fairly basic tramcars were built in 1904 by the Loughborough-based Brush tram builder in 1904. The tram is standing in front of a row of shops which were constructed in about 1901 between Windmill Lane and the entrance to the coke yard. Amazingly, these buildings have survived into the twenty-first century despite the construction of the Windmill Shopping Centre. (D.R. Harvey Collection)

On an Edwardian summer's day in about 1906, B&M single-deck Car 59, a Kyotts Lake Road Works-built closed-combination tram with a monitor-style roof and an 8ft 6in Lycett & Conaty Radial truck, is working on the wrong track towards Smethwick. This is because of road works blocking the track between Waterloo Road and the distant Claremont Road. On the right is the Gospel Hall with its tall gabled roof which is adjacent to the entrance to the Windmill Lane steam tram coking yard. (J.H. Taylforth)

Looking towards Cape Hill from the Smethwick end of the High Street in about 1902 is a B&M Kitson steam tram pulling a double-deck trailer. Standing at the top of Bearwood Hill, the tram is travelling on the Smethwick-bound track at Windmill Lane. On the left is the impressive Market Place building which later became the Co-operative Society, while the tall trees behind the tram are elms which gave their name to the large eighteenth-century house which was demolished in 1906. (Commercial Postcard via A. Maxam)

At Windmill Lane Birmingham & Midland Tramways Co. built a coke yard in 1885 for its steam trams which also had four tracks for servicing engines. Standing outside this facility is Kitson Standard-style locomotive 26, dating from 1898 and assembled by BMT. It is attached to a sixty-two-seat open-sided canopy-topped single-ended double-decker with semi-enclosed leading balconies which also date from 1898. The journey time from Birmingham to Dudley was one hour and ten minutes, hourly between 8 a.m. and 9 p.m., with shorts in both directions to Spon Lane and, as here, to Windmill Lane. (D.R. Harvey Collection)

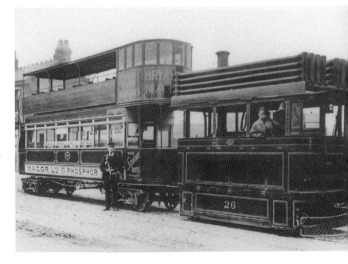

On 12 April 1939, Birmingham Car 88, a UEC-built former Radial-truck four-wheel tramcar built in 1906, travels towards Dudley on the 87 service. It has descended Bearwood Hill from Cape Hill. On the left is the lodge and impressive entrance gates to Victoria Park, which was opened to the public on 7 September 1895 due to it being funded by the local glass factory owner Sir James Chance, Bart. The tram is about to overtake the parked 1936 Armstrong-Siddeley Standard 17 saloon. (H.B. Priestley)

About four years after it was constructed, one of the original open-top Brush-built company trams from the 1-12 series of 1904 passes the original Red Cow public house in High Street just beyond Smethwick Council House. The tramcar is heading towards West Smethwick and Oldbury. The ivy-covered house on the left was at the junction with Watery Lane, but was soon demolished in order to widen the main road. (A. Maxam Collection)

Working on the 446 route to Oldbury is Ailsa B55-10, 4745 (JOV 745P), which was one of thirty allocated to Oldbury Garage. These front-engined buses had Alexander H44/35F bodies which had a capacity three more than a standard rear-engined 'Fleetline'. Known as 'the whistling buses' because of the noise made by their turbo-chargers, the Ailsa was a product of Volvo. WMPTE had fifty-three of these splendid buses and were at the point of ordering another batch when the 'support local industry' lobby stopped the order and yet more of the obsolete Leyland 'Fleetlines' were ordered. 4745 is seen here in High Street, West Smethwick, near Rolfe Street in October 1982. (D.R. Harvey)

The George Inn, selling the locally brewed Mitchells & Butlers ales and stouts, was in High Street on the corner of Brasshouse Lane. The pub was demolished in 1981 to make way for Tollhouse Way, a dual-carriageway bypass. In September 1939 Car 159 is travelling to Oldbury on the 86 route. Within a few days this UEC-bodied tramcar, built in 1907 along with the other forty-nine of the class shedded at West Smethwick, was placed in store and broken up by Cashmores early in 1940. (Newman College)

On its way along High Street, Smethwick, on 3 April 1989 is 2815 (B815 AOP). This MCW 'Metrobus' Mk II DR 102/27 had a Metro-Cammell H43/30F body. The bus entered service during November 1984 and was eventually taken out of service at the end of 2008. The bus is working on the 87 route to Dudley and is being followed by a Travel West Midlands Leyland National. On the right are the early Edwardian premises, standing on the western side of the High Street, which survived the construction of the Tollhouse Way bypass. (D.R. Harvey)

High Street, Smethwick, was a bustling shopping centre throughout the years of tramcar operation. It was the 1960s planning blight on the buildings to the left of the tramcar caused by the proposed Tollhouse Way that caused the decline in the area, only arrested when the quality of the early twentieth-century premises on the right was eventually realised and they were given a 'make-over'. Birmingham & Midland Tramways Car 46, in its final mid-1920s condition, fitted with a front vestibule screen to partially protect the driver (or motorman), heads away from the St Paul's Road junction as it proceeds through the shopping centre towards Cape Hill and Birmingham. (D.R. Harvey Collection)

11

ST PAUL'S ROAD
TO OLDBURY

Posing at the St Paul's Road terminus in Smethwick with the driver and conductor as well as the two smocked young girls, it looks as though this was an important occasion. It is probable that this is 24 November 1904 which was the opening day of Birmingham & Midland electric tram operations between Lionel Street in Birmingham and Dudley. Car 7 was one of twelve of the original 1-18 batch of tramcars fitted with 'Bellamy'-type top-covers originally designed by the Liverpool General Manager, C.R. Bellamy, and is mounted on a rigid Brush AA-type truck. (D.R. Harvey Collection)

Because of blackout regulations, street furniture, kerb edgings and the vehicles all had white-painted edges. Car 150, a UEC-built tram dating from 1907, given a vestibule and re-trucked on Brush Peckham trucks, picks up passengers in Oldbury Road. The tram is working on the 86 route to Oldbury late in September 1939, just before the abandonment of the Dudley services along 'The Track'. On the left is St Paul's Road with the tall Empire Theatre on the left. Built in 1910, from 1930 until 1957 the Empire was used solely as a cinema. (R.T. Wilson)

Car 98 works along the interlaced track on Oldbury Road on 30 September 1939. It is travelling towards St Paul's Road having left the terminus of the 85 route at Spon Lane, just over ½ mile away. Behind the tram and beyond the petrol station is the magnificent Galton Bridge. This was designed by Thomas Telford and was opened in 1828 with a huge 150ft span made of cast-iron some 71ft above Telford's Birmingham Level of the Birmingham Canal Navigation. On the left is a sign for Palethorpes' sausages, at this time based locally in Tipton. (L.W. Perkins)

On 2 July 1938, standing at the 85 route terminus in Oldbury Road, is ex-Radial truck, UEC-bodied Car 102. In the distance is Spon Lane with the derelict Spon Lane Tavern waiting to be demolished. Until November 1929 single-deck B&M trams also worked along Oldbury Road on a circular service using both Spon Lane and Bromford Lane to link Oldbury and West Bromwich. (Birmingham Central Reference Library)

Above: A freshly repainted Brush-bodied SOS FEDD waits in the bus bay in Oldbury Road, in the
bus lay-by outside the Spon Croft public house. This pub was opened on 7 June 1935, replacing
the eighteenth-century Spon Lane Tavern. The Spon Croft closed in 1995 and was demolished in
1999. 2372 (FHA 876) is probably working on the B85 route to Spon Lane as the driver isn't in his
cab and there are very few passengers on this forward entrance double-decker. 2372 was one of the
last six SOS FEDDs to remain in service, being withdrawn in December 1960. The bus is carrying
an advertisement for Atkinson's Ales, founded in 1855 and based at the Park Brewery in Aston.
In 1959 Atkinson's were acquired by Mitchells & Butlers. The bus is parked alongside a typical
wartime bus shelter consisting of tubular scaffolding poles and a corrugated cover purporting to be
a roof! (A.N. Porter)

Opposite: Travelling along a section of single-line track in Oldbury Road near to the West
Smethwick Depot in the mid-1920s is a Birmingham & Midland Co. tram. Top-covered Car 4
has a style of driver's windscreen which was fitted to many of the associated Black Country Co.
trams from about 1914, by which time this Brush-bodied tram was about ten years old. To the left,
the factory building is part of the Chance Glassworks. Chance Bros was founded in 1824 in Spon
Lane, Smethwick. During the nineteenth century it became one of the most important glassworks
in Britain. It manufactured sheet glass, including the panes for the Crystal Palace of 1851, window
glass in different colours and optical glass including the lenses for lighthouses. Most of the furnaces
and cones were demolished in the late 1940s, though the 1830s factory buildings are being slowly
restored as an industrial heritage site. (D.R. Harvey Collection)

Above: Standing at the entrance to West Smethwick Depot on a miserable Friday is Car 74. It is 23 September 1939 and the Second World War has been going for nearly three weeks, though the tram is still without any wartime blackout white edges. This UEC-built tram entered service in August 1906 with top-covers enabling the top deck to be used by twenty-eight passengers in inclement weather. Car 74 is facing the Birmingham direction as it works on the 87 route from Dudley. Opposite the depot was Chance's huge glass manufactory as well as the Britannia public house whose beers must have slaked the thirst of literally millions of glass foundry workers during the century or so in which Chances were making glass. (J.S. Webb)

Opposite above: Posed in West Smethwick Depot yard is B&M steam locomotive 22, built by Thomas Green in 1886. It was rebuilt in 1898 with an iron cab and Cannon condensers coupled to Starbuck open-sided top-canopy-covered bogie trailer 22, built in 1886 as a sixty-two-seat double-decker. The steam tram operation between Birmingham and Dudley ended on 23 November 1904 with the new electric trams taking over on the following day. (D.R. Harvey Collection)

Opposite below: The Birmingham & Midland Tramway Co. acquired a 3½-acre site beyond the Spon Lane junction on the boundary of West Smethwick and Oldbury. West Smethwick Depot was opened in the summer of 1885 and operated steam trams until they were replaced by electric trams on 24 November 1904. An immaculately painted Car 88 stands in the vast expanse of West Smethwick's depot yard in about 1929. This UEC-bodied former Radial car of 1907 was by now fitted with a Brush Peckham P35 8ft 6in-long truck. Although the depot had a capacity of only forty-four trams, its yard could accommodate up to sixty more. This was particularly useful after the Dudley Road tram services were abandoned when the depot's final duty was to store nearly all of the surviving 71-class trams before they were scrapped on site, a task which was completed in April 1940, some seven months after the abandonment. (D.R. Harvey Collection)

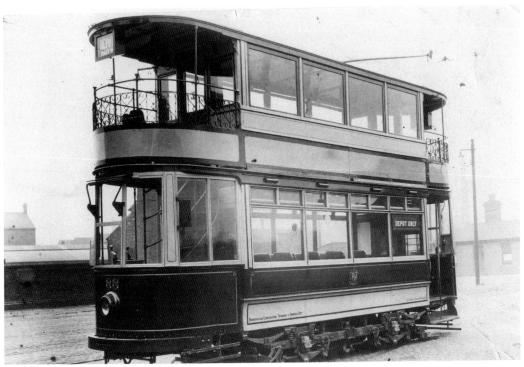

In the summer of 1938 no less than eleven tramcars stand in the entrance to West Smethwick Depot. Ten of the trams belong to the 71–220 class of UEC top-covered former Radial-truck four-wheel trams dating from 1906. From left to right these tramcars are: 129, 195, 153, 94, 107, 151, 136, 193, 192 and 186. The exception is Car 490, on the extreme left, which is former CBT 'Aston'-type Car 227, the only one here to start its life as an open-topper. The tram depot had three gable-ended sheds with the single-track entrance on Oldbury Road leading into a fan of eleven roads serving the car sheds and a capacity for forty-four trams under cover. (R.T. Coxon)

Negotiating the Rood End Road traffic island in Oldbury Road is 4372 (VHA 372). This BMMO D7 had a Metro-Cammell H32/26R body that had entered service in 1955. It was withdrawn in August 1969 having spent the whole of its career working from Oldbury Garage. The bus is seen here working on the B87 route approaching Oldbury on its way to Dudley in about 1966. Midland Red was the only operator beyond Spon Lane on either the B86 or B87 routes on a ten-minute headway. (A.D. Broughall)

Above: Approaching Oldbury in Birmingham Road in September 2006 is one of the brand new route-dedicated Volvo B7TLs with a Wright H43/29F body. 4709 (BU 06 CXC), working on the 87 route, has just passed beneath the M5 motorway as it passes Manchester Street. Behind the bus is the factory site of Metal Sections who exported bus body frames all around the world. Their advertising slogan was 'a bus in a box'. (D.R. Harvey)

Right: Towards the Market Place end of Birmingham Street, the road through the middle of Oldbury was sufficiently narrow that the tram tracks were laid so close together that trams travelling in opposite directions could not pass each other. In later years this section of the line was controlled by signal lights. Travelling into Oldbury from Birmingham is B&M open-top Car 19. This tram was the first of the company's Brush-built open-top four-wheelers known as 'Aston'-type cars. They were delivered in November 1904 and fitted with 8ft 6in wheelbases and Lycett & Conaty Radial axle trucks which, like the BCT 71-class trams, were re-trucked due to their poor riding qualities. Behind the tram is the Junction public house on the corner of the distant Unity Place and Birmingham Street. (Commercial Postcard)

Travelling across Oldbury Market Place is BCT Car 80. It is working on the 87 route on 23 September 1939, just one week before the tram route was abandoned. The tram has just left Birmingham Street on the left and is about to pass into Freeth Street alongside Oldbury Council House. Standing in the Market Place is a West Bromwich Corporation Dennis 'Lancet' while behind it is a brand new Midland Red SOS FEDD. The single-decker is working on the former B&M single-deck circular tram service, having come from West Bromwich by way of Bromford Lane on the left where the curve of the granite sets lie abandoned. (J.S. Webb)

The B86 and B87 bus services did not use Oldbury Bus Station. The B86 terminated in Oldbury but went into Inkerman Street at the back of Oldbury Council House. 3501 (MHA 501), a 1949 vintage BMMO D5 with a Brush H30/26R open rear platform body, lies over in the bus lay-by before returning to pick up again in Freeth Street opposite the Council House. (D. Wilson)

Standing in Oldbury Bus Station in 1985 is 4747 (JOV 747P). This was one of the fifty splendid Ailsa B55–10s with Alexander H44/35F bodies dating from 1976. These buses had turbo-charged 6.7-litre Volvo TD70 engines which made a splendid whistling noise when accelerating. They had relatively short lives, being sold to Harrow Bus in 1987 as being non-standard. 4747 is working on the 88 service from Birmingham to Oldbury by way of Londonderry, in deepest suburban Smethwick. (Millbrook House)

Picking up passengers alongside the newly rebuilt Oldbury Bus Station in Halesowen Street, opposite the huge Sava Shopping Centre in the middle of Oldbury, is West Midland Travel's 2904 (C904 FON). This MCW 'Metrobus' Mk II DR102/48 had a Metro-Cammell H43/30F body which, surprisingly, had three seats less in the lower saloon than their Daimler/Leyland 'Fleetline' predecessors. 2904 is working on the 87 route on 7 July 1998. (D.R. Harvey)

Left: Facing Dudley in Freeth Street alongside Oldbury Council House is UEC-bodied ex-Radial-truck four-wheel Car 92. The impressive Council House had its foundation stone laid on 19 May 1890 and was distinguished by its turreted tower on the corner of Halesowen Street. The tram is working on the 87 route in the last days of tramcar operation on 'The Track' in September 1939. It was in many ways a shame that this inter-urban tram service was abandoned when it might have so easily been reprieved because of the need to conserve the scarce wartime fuel supplies. (R.T. Wilson)

Below: Working to Dudley on the 87 route is a 1955 vintage BMMO D7, 4459 (XHA 459), fitted with a Metro-Cammell H37/26RD body. The route number suggests that this is after the closure of the Corporation's Rosebery Street Garage when the B prefix on the route number was dropped. The D7 is also alongside the Council House in Freeth Street, Oldbury, and is standing at the utilitarian bus shelter which, although similar to those found in Birmingham, had their poles painted black and white. (D.R. Harvey Collection)

Standing on the forecourt of Oldbury Garage in about 1958 is this rather tired-looking Brush H30/26F-bodied SOS FEDD, 2268 (FHA 250), built in 1939. These buses were the last batch of pre-war SOS double-deckers to enter service which, with the exception of the rather basic single-skinned upper saloon ceiling, had very well appointed interiors. The complete batch of fifty buses was specifically used from new as part of the tramway conversion programme on 'The Track' when that took place on 30 September 1939. This name is still used today for the Dudley Road, Smethwick, Oldbury and Dudley route. Many of these excellent buses spent their entire lives allocated to Oldbury Garage, which in the case of 2268 was almost twenty-one years. (R.H.G. Simpson Collection)

Oldbury Garage opened on 12 April 1937 and had a capacity of seventy buses. The 7¾-ton BMMO D5s were regular performers on the Dudley Road services from the early 1950s and were operated by Oldbury Garage. They were the nearest bus to a standard Birmingham Corporation vehicle as they were fifty-six-seaters and had open rear platforms. Brush-bodied 3549 (MHA 549) was withdrawn in 1964 and is seen parked on the garage forecourt shortly before it was taken out of service. Displaying the B86

route number, the D5s originally worked alongside Oldbury's SOS FEDDs which had arrived at the garage for the Midland Red share of the replacement Dudley Road bus services. 3549 is parked alongside two of the later Metro-Cammell-bodied BMMO D7s, with 4472 (XHA 472) on the left and 4529 (XHA 529) standing in the garage entrance. (A.D. Broughall)

Parked in front of Oldbury Garage in about 1974, with Birchley Island on the A4123 Wolverhampton New Road behind, is the first production BMMO D9 double-decker which entered service in February 1960. 4849 (849 KHA) had been taken over by West Midlands PTE on 4 December 1973. This 30ft-long seventy-two-seater is still in the all-over Midland Red livery, but has now received a red-backed WM fablon fleetname. Parked alongside it are a pair of former Birmingham CT Crossley-bodied Daimler CVG6s. (D.R. Harvey Collection)

Oldbury Garage opened on 12 April 1937 and closed in early 1986. Its final allocation of buses included about half of the 1976 batch of WMPTE-owned Ailsa B55–10s with Alexander bodies. These buses revolutionised the operation of the 87 route as they had a good turn of speed and were quick off the mark. They had engines mounted at the front opposite the entrance doors, and with their turbo-chargers working hard, theses vehicles were known by all who travelled on them as 'the whistling buses'. Parked on the forecourt of Oldbury Garage in July 1984 are two of these buses, 4753 (JOV 753P) and 4746 (JOV 746P). It is worthy of note that the destination display reads BLACK HEATH rather than BLACKHEATH. (D.R. Harvey)

12

BRADES VILLAGE
TO DUDLEY

Opposite above: In recent years the Richardson Bros have become well-known Black Country figures because of their entrepreneurial re-development of the Round Oak Steelworks into the huge Merry Hill Shopping Centre. Thirty years earlier the Richardson's began dealing in and scrapping buses in a yard alongside Dudley Road in Brades Village, adjacent to the Gower Branch of the Birmingham Canal. In April 1962 they purchased from Birmingham City Transport some thirty-two Daimler CVA6s, fourteen Daimler CVG6s, three Daimler CVD6s and one Brush-bodied Leyland 'Titan' PD2/1. Of these fifty buses, fifteen were sold for further service. Most of the buses visible are GOE-registered Daimler CVA6s, while there is also a brand new Guy 'Big J' eight-wheel lorry chassis in the foreground. (L. Mason)

Opposite below: Former Radial Car 80 is about to leave the passing loop in Dudley Road East, near Brades Village, working from Oldbury on the 87 route towards Dudley in about 1937. Behind the tram is derelict land, laying testament to the terrible decline in the primary and heavy engineering industries of the Black Country since the end of the First World War. (K. Lane)

Below: Again in Dudley Road East near Lower City Road, about thirty years later, is a Birmingham-bound Midland Red bus. BMMO D7 4504 (XHA 504) is working on the B87 route in an area of Brades Village which at this time was a landscape of dereliction with only a few clusters of houses to interrupt the acres of waste and abandoned industrial land. The bus is carrying an advertisement for M&B's Sam Brown ale, which was a popular bottled brown ale in the 1960s. (A.D. Broughall)

At The Boat Inn, Tividale, the trams turned left into Tipton Road and climbed over the BCN's Old Main Line canal. This was another example on 'The Track' where there was a single-line track that was controlled by traffic signals. The original early nineteenth-century Boat Inn and the old cottages stand in the background as open-balconied Car 129 travels towards Tividale Depot and Dudley, employed on the 87 route on 24 June 1939. (R.T. Coxon)

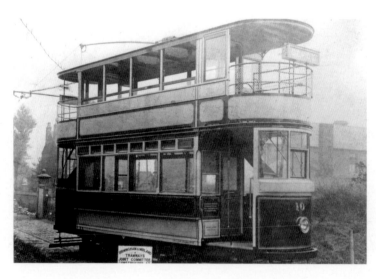

Standing on the trackwork at the entrance to Tividale depot is tram 10. This tramcar was constructed at the Tividale Works in August 1914 for the Birmingham District section of the Birmingham & Midland Tramways Joint Committee. These 8ft 6in semi-radial-trucked double-deckers were fitted with BTH GE60 35hp motors and had hand and rheostatic braking. These were the first trams built new for the Black Country systems with drivers vestibule screens while the open balcony was fitted with wing windows which helped to eliminate draughts. Car 10 was the prototype tram belonging to the last of the 'Aston'-type tramcars which had been in production in various guises since 1904. It sat twenty-two inside and under the protection of the four-windowed top-cover another twenty-six passengers upstairs. This tram was one of the thirty-eight company cars which were briefly hired to Birmingham Corporation from April until September 1928 to cover for BCT's shortage of tramcars after their take-over of the Dudley Road 'Track' services. (B&MTJC Official Photograph)

In Dudley Road West, Tividale, 4708 (BU 06 CXB), one of the Dudley Road route dedicated Volvo B7TLs with Wright H43/29F bodies, is travelling towards Burnt Tree Island on the outskirts of Dudley on the 87 route. On 14 August 2006, when only a few days old, this bus is picking up passengers at the Hill Road bus stop outside a group of 1930s former council houses. (D.R. Harvey)

Travelling towards Dudley is former Radial-truck Car 136 on the last day of operation on 30 September 1939. It is passing rows of Victorian houses and the entrance to the now closed former B&M Tividale Works and Depot. Behind the tram is a parked Dudley-registered 1939 Morris Eight Series E. Tividale Depot had been opened on 1 January 1907 and was closed in March 1930. The disused track into the depot remained in position, as did the overhead. The overhead was used for feeder purposes from the sub-station inside the depot yard until the final closure of the 87 tram route. The state of the trackwork in the Tividale area by this time was not good, and, coupled to the hard-riding characteristics of these 71-class tramcars with their wooden seats, did not make for a comfortable ride. (R.T. Coxon)

These open-top tramcars were built by Brush in 1904 and fitted with the quite short Brush AA 6ft 6in-long trucks, which would have given a tail-wagging ride on anything other than good quality tracks. The tram is parked in Tividale Depot yard in 1921. The tram was at one time fitted with a short Bellamy top-cover, though this was removed before the car was transferred to the South Staffordshire section. The tram is fitted with a very basic driver's window which left the sides of the vestibules open to the elements. (W. Gratwicke)

Climbing Tividale Road, with the tower of St Michael's Church overlooking Tividale tram works in the distance, is a company car. The tram is approaching Burnt Tree within a couple of years of the end of company operations. This Brush-built 'Aston'-type tram built in 1904 was originally an open-topper but was extensively rebuilt with a Tividale-built top-cover, roller blind destination boxes over the vestibule and a 35 or 40hp motor. On 1 April 1928 the Birmingham & Midland operation of the Birmingham–Oldbury–Dudley route was taken over by Birmingham Corporation. (R. Bennett)

13

DUDLEY

Opposite above: The junction between Dudley Road and Tividale Road at Burnt Tree Crossing, where the still fairly recently built New Birmingham Road avoided Dudley town centre, was where the 'mainline' from West Bromwich met 'The Track' from Oldbury. In about 1938, on the right of the junction, coming from Tividale Road, is open-balcony UEC-bodied Car 154. The tram is working on the 87 route. On the left is Car 532, operating on the 74 service from West Bromwich. It is a sunny day and the driver of this UEC-bodied bogie car has extended the vestibule sun visor. (W.A. Camwell)

Opposite below: The tramcars coming from West Bromwich travelled from Dudley Port to Burnt Tree where they crossed the Birmingham New Road. This had been opened by HRH the Prince of Wales on 2 November 1927. On a miserable day in March 1939 a UEC-bodied bogie totally enclosed tram, Car 521, is about to join the tram tracks which brought the 87 route from Oldbury to Dudley. From this Burnt Tree junction to the terminus at the bottom of Castle Hill, from 30 March 1903, the original South Staffordshire cars were able to run over B&M-owned track. The Victorian houses on the left were demolished in about 1991 when a very large Tesco supermarket was built on the site. (R.T. Coxon)

Below: In 1948, West Bromwich Corporation purchased ten Daimler CVG6s. These buses were fitted with Metro-Cammell bodies which were built to a design that was a cross between the contemporary Birmingham style and the pre-war Edinburgh type. Bus 149 (DEA 549), looking very smart, being freshly repainted and having a splendid set of knobbly front tyres, stands at Burnt Tree Island on Birmingham Road, working on the 74 route. Behind the lorry is the garage which stood on the triangle between Tividale Road and Burnt Tree. (D. Williams)

Above: Standing in Birmingham Road at the Dudley Station terminus is a steam tram working on the Handsworth to Dudley route. The steam locomotive was one of the 3–12 batch built in 1883 by Beyer Peacock. The fifty-two-seat plate-framed bogie car had been built by Falcon of Loughborough in late 1883. The steam ream route reached Dudley on 12 October 1885, from Great Bridge, and lasted until its conversion to electric traction on 30 May 1903. (H. Whitcombe Collection)

Opposite above: Examples of the two very different types of Birmingham Corporation trams stand at the Dudley terminus. The tram terminus for both the 74 service from West Bromwich and the 87 route from Smethwick was located at some rather splendid passenger shelters. This was between the distant Midland Red garage and the bottom of Trindle Road, almost directly opposite the entrance to Dudley Station located on the opposite side of the road. On 16 June 1938, Car 219, an open-balcony former Radial-trucked tram allocated to West Smethwick Depot waits for customers on the 87 route. Behind is totally enclosed bogie Car 544, which is working on the 74 route. (R. T. Coxon)

Opposite below: Journey's end! It was a 9-mile journey on the 74 route from Birmingham to Dudley, and on 23 October 1938, Car 607, a Brush totally enclosed bogie tram, has just arrived at the terminus at the bottom of Castle Hill, with the recently rebuilt Station Hotel on the far corner of Trindle Road. Car 607 stands on the bridge over the railway line opposite Dudley Station. Beyond it, parked as far up the surviving track as possible, is Birmingham's last tramcar, the Brush lightweight Car 843, which was being used on the extensive LRTL Tour, which covered every part of the Birmingham tramway system. Standing further up Castle Hill opposite the Dudley Hippodrome Theatre is a Midland Red SOS FEDD, probably working on the service to Brierley Hill or Stourbridge. (L. W. Perkins)

The terminus of all the Birmingham bus services that ended at Dudley was outside the Midland Red bus garage. This building, housing the garage offices as well as the booking and enquiry shops, was originally opened on 2 August 1929 and was located at the bottom of the distant Castle Hill, opposite Tipton Road. It is appropriate that in August 1952, not long before Dudley's first bus station was opened in Fisher Street, that the only buses in sight are those owned by Midland Red. Waiting to start its journey back to Birmingham by way of Oldbury on the B87 route is Brush H30/26F-bodied SOS FEDD 2380 (FHA884), dating from 1939, having been bought specifically to replace the trams on 'The Track'. Outside the Midland Red premises is a 1936 FEDD, in this case 1783 (BHA 381), which had a metal-framed MCCW body. (R. Knibbs)

Parked outside Midland Red's Dudley Bus Garage in about 1952 are two of Birmingham's Leyland-bodied Leyland 'Titan' PD2/1s. 2150 (JOJ 150), and behind it 2148 (JOJ 148), have unloaded outside the garage. They will in turn move forward and negotiate the Tipton Road traffic island before loading next to the entrance to Dudley Town FCs ground. These buses were about 5in lower than the standard Birmingham double-decker, which was most noticeable when they were parked next to a bus such as the SOS FEDD, parked opposite. This is Midland Red's SOS FEDD 2363 (FHA 867), working on the B87 route. The garage was closed in 1993 as the site was required for the new junction of the Dudley Southern Bypass at the large Castle Gate traffic island. (E. Chitham)

The original allocation for buses at Dudley Garage was for about thirty vehicles, but as services proliferated, the poorly designed undercover accommodation became inadequate. Buses frequently had to reverse out into Birmingham Road, which occasionally caused traffic accidents. In the post-war years the land between the railway cutting alongside Trindle Road and Wolverton Road was acquired for outdoor parking, and in October 1989 three West Midlands Travel Metro-Cammell-bodied Leyland 'Fleetline' FE30AGRs, 6428 (NOC428R), 6720 (SDA 720S) and 6498 (NOC 498R), stand in the garage yard. (D.R. Harvey)

Occasionally, buses working on the 74 route were parked in Wolverton Road alongside the Midland Red Garage in Dudley. 229 (EOG 229) is parked next to the garage facing Birmingham Road in 1948. The bus is a Metro-Cammell-bodied Leyland 'Titan' TD6c, the 'c' standing for torque convertor, which was an early form of semi-automatic gearbox. This meant that the driver had a three-position gear lever with a position for 'torque' which took the bus up to about 20mph, at which point the driver pulled the gear lever back into the 'direct drive' position taking the bus on to its top speed. There was also a reverse gear. The gearbox had to be lubricated using a paraffin and oil mixture and the header tank can clearly be seen on the front bulkhead next to the side light. This 1939-vintage bus had about another four years service with BCT in front of it. (D. Griffiths)

Standing beyond Dudley Bus Garage in Birmingham Road are two West Bromwich Corporation Daimler COG6s dating from 1939. These buses were purchased as part of the West Bromwich tram replacement scheme. 95 (AEA 25) and 85 (AEA 15) are both resting, having arrived from Birmingham on the 74 service. The destination box on 95 has already been turned around prior to returning to the city. Behind the bus is the traffic island at the top of Tipton Road. (M.J.C. Dare)

The last of Birmingham City Transport's fifty Leyland-bodied Leyland 'Titan' PD2/1s of 1949 was 2180 (JOJ 180). In September 1952 this bus stands at the Dudley terminus of the 74 route alongside the Bundy Clock, opposite Midland Red's Dudley Bus Garage. It is still fitted with its original trafficator arms. The driver of the Leyland is standing alongside his charge as he waits for his departure time to come round. Just visible standing at the bus shelter alongside the Tipton Road entrance to Dudley Station is a BMMO D5B. (R. Knibbs)

In earlier days an almost new large South Staffordshire maximum traction bogie Car 23, built by Brush early in 1903 with a capacity of seventy passengers, waits at the bottom of Castle Hill in about 1910. These trams led with their bogie pony wheels, which resulted in the trams being prone to derailment on poor track. This tram is working on the Dudley to Handsworth service and is standing in front of the original Victorian Station Hotel which was demolished in 1936 and replaced by the building which thrives today. On the right is the forested Castle Hill which has on it Dudley's famous Norman castle dating from around 1071. (D.R. Harvey Collection)

On 6 March 2007 a Diamond Bus double-decker has descended Castle Hill, working on the 74 route. This was when the company was briefly owned by the Go-Ahead Group who brought in a number of these Volvo 'Olympian' B10Ms with Northern Counties seventy-eight-seat bodies from their London operation. 907 (P907 RYO) has just overtaken a TWM Mercedes-Benz 0405N single-decker, 1704 (V704 MOA), both buses vying for trade on the 74 route. Behind the double-decker is the 1937 Station Hotel building, which claims to be the most haunted building in Dudley. (D.R. Harvey)

West Bromwich Corporation's 171 (GEA 171), a 1952 vintage Daimler CVG6 with a Weymann H30/26R body, speeds down Castle Hill having just passed the entrance to Dudley Zoo. The bus has just left the original Dudley Bus Station and is heading back to Birmingham on the 74 route. *A Weekend with Lulu* was the show at the Dudley Hippodrome Theatre in about 1967. (P. Yeomans)

On a really awful day in the pouring rain, 6790 (SDA 790S), a MCW-bodied Leyland 'Fleetline' FE30AGR, leaves the Station Hotel behind as it climbs Castle Hill. 6790 entered service in April 1978 and is working on the 74 route in about 1985. It is approaching the turn into Birmingham Street where the buses from Birmingham unloaded. (D.R. Harvey)

The unloading point for the 74 route in Dudley was at the bottom end of Birmingham Street up the steep hill opposite the entrance to Dudley Zoo and Castle. On the right is the parking area for Midland Red's Dudley town local services. The parking of buses on this hill caused several accidents when buses rolled away. In about 1965, one of the long-lived Leyland 'Titan' PD2/1s with Leyland H30/26R bodies, 2168 (JOJ 168), has unloaded and is waiting for its crew to return from the café in Fisher Street. (J.H. Blake)

Above: In the final year of municipal bus operation in 1969, Hockley Garage used their latest two-door Park Royal-bodied Daimler 'Fleetline' CRG6LXs on the 74 route. 3789 (NOV 789G) is parked in Birmingham Street having unloaded its passengers. On the skyline one of the towers of Dudley Castle stands out at the top of the distant Castle Hill. (D.R. Harvey Collection)

Opposite above: In 1970, not long after the West Midlands PTE takeover, like the trams just over forty years earlier, two buses stand in Birmingham Street having arrived at their terminus in Dudley. On the left is a former West Bromwich Corporation bus working on the 74 route. 258 (258 TEA) is a 1964 Daimler CVG6 with a Metro-Cammell 'Orion' H37/29R body. Standing in the Midland Red parking area, having worked on the 87 route from Smethwick and Oldbury, is a by now fairly elderly Midland Red BMMO D7, 4371 (VHA 371). (C.W. Routh)

Opposite below: Turning into Fisher Street in order to load up before heading back to West Bromwich and Birmingham is 2191 (JOJ 191). This Park Royal-bodied Leyland 'Titan' PD2/1 is working on the 74 route in about 1966. The bus entered service on 1 November 1949 and almost survived into WMPTE days, not being finally withdrawn until July 1969. These buses did not have the standard BCT straight staircase which on other routes would have caused problems for passengers and conductors alike, but because the West Bromwich buses which jointly operated the 74 also had angled staircases, their use was not really a problem. (D.R. Harvey Collection)

Above: Dudley Bus Station was opened in 1952 in Fisher Street which had the advantage of running at right angles to the hill in Birmingham Street. This enabled the buses to Birmingham to load up on the flat. Standing alongside the concrete bus shelters and next to the Bundy Clock is one of Hockley Garage's Daimler CVG6s. This bus had a Crossley H30/25R body and entered service on 1 March 1954, making it two years younger than the bus station. In August 1960 this bus was fitted with fluorescent front destination lights. 3165 is working on the 74 route. (C. Carter)

Opposite above: When the new Dudley Bus Station was built in about 1989, the buses coming from Castle Hill had their own dedicated entrance off Birmingham Street. In March 1995, Mk I MCW 'Metrobus' 2071 (BOK 71V) stands in the setting-down point, working on the 87 route. After the brief ownership due to a management buy-out, this bus is wearing the short-lived West Midlands fleetname, which also gave the operating garage. Thus, 2071 is carrying 'WM West Bromwich' on its lower panels. (D.R. Harvey)

Opposite below: In January 2009 it was announced that a £3.5 million project to replace the twenty-year-old Dudley Bus Station would be implemented within the next couple of years. On 4 October 2006 a brand new Volvo B7Tl with a Wright H43/29F body is about to leave the parking area to run round to its pick-up stand on the far side of Dudley Bus Station. As previously mentioned these buses with their distinctive lower windscreens have been given the nickname of 'Nokia buses' as they resemble the front of a Nokia mobile phone. (D.R. Harvey)

Other titles published by The History Press

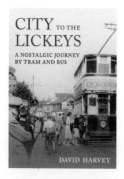

City to the Lickeys: A Nostalgic Journey by Tram and Bus
DAVID HARVEY

For many hardworking Brummies a day trip to the Lickey Hills was their only entertainment or leisure activity. From the spring of 1924 until the mid-1950s, a trip there on the Rednal tram for a 5*d* ticket became the only holiday many people could afford. Take a journey along Bristol Road and Pershore Road from the city centre to Rednal and Rubery and to Cotteridge by tram and bus; look at the street scenes from a different time and see why the Lickey Hills became such an attraction.

ISBN 978 0 7524 4697 4

Top-Deck Travel: A History of Britain's Open-Top Buses
PHILIP C. MILES

This illustrated history charts the development of the open-top bus, from the early 1900s when buses ordinarily had an open top-deck to the bustling sightseeing operations so popular around the world today, recalling many operators along the way who have since been relegated to the annals of history.

ISBN 978 0 7524 5137 4

Luton Corporation Transport
PETER ROSE

Covering the history of municipal transport in Luton from the first horse-drawn buses and the town's electric trams through to the sale of the undertaking to United Counties, the bus company which dominated services in the rest of Bedfordshire, this fully illustrated book will have a nostalgic appeal to all who have lived and worked in Luton during the Corporation era and beyond to many bus enthusiasts nationwide.

ISBN 978 0 7524 4913 5

The London Bus Story
JOHN CHRISTOPHER

Buses have been operating on London's streets since 1829, originally with horse-drawn omnibuses, and the London Omnibus Company was founded in 1855 to regulate the various services. More recent innovations such as the 'bendy' bus have not been popular, but today the practicality of pushchair and wheelchair access has consigned the Routemaster to a nostalgic, but much-loved, position.

ISBN 978 0 7524 5084 1

Visit our website and discover thousands of other History Press books.

www.thehistorypress.co.uk